THE MAGIC OF THE

MEDITERRANEAN

Sun-drenched recipes from the shores of southern Europe

CONSULTANT EDITOR

DONATELLA MANCINI

LORENZ BOOKS

First published in 1999 by Lorenz Books

© Anness Publishing Limited 1999

Lorenz Books is an imprint of
Anness Publishing Limited
Hermes House
88-89 Blackfriars Road
London SE1 8HA

This edition distributed in Canada by
Raincoast Books
8680 Cambie Street
Vancouver
British Columbia V6P 6M9

ISBN 0 7548 0053 9

A CIP catalogue record for this book is available from the British Library

Publisher: Joanna Lorenz
Project Editor: Sarah Duffin
Designers: Ian Sandom and Nigel Partridge
Illustrations: Madeleine David
Recipes: Catherine Atkinson, Carla Capalbo, Jacqueline Clark, Frances Cleary, Carole Clements, Roz Denny,
Matthew Drennan, Joanna Farrow, Christine France, Silvana Franco, Sarah Gates, Shirley Gill, Carole Handslip, Judy Jackson,
Soheila Kimberley, Patricia Lousada, Norma MacMillan, Sue Maggs, Sarah Maxwell, Janice Murfitt, Annie Nichols,
Angela Nilsen, Jenny Stacey, Liz Trigg, Laura Washburn, Steven Wheeler and Elizabeth Wolf-Cohen
Photographers: William Adams-Lingwood, Karl Adamson, Edward Allwright, Steve Baxter,
James Duncan, Michelle Garrett, Amanda Heywood, Tim Hill, Don Last, Patrick McLeavey and Michael Michaels
Jacket photography: Nicki Dowey
Stylists: Madelaine Brehaut, Frances Cleary, Nicola Fowler, Michelle Garrett, Teresa Goldfinch, Hilary Guy, Amanda Heywood,
Carole Handslip, Cara Hobday, Clare Louise Hunt, Maria Kelly, Sarah Maxwell, Blake Minton, Kirsty Rawlings and Fiona Tillett.

Printed and bound in Singapore

For all recipes, quantities are given in both metric and imperial measures, and, where appropriate,
measures are also given in standard cups and spoons. Follow one set, but not a mixture,
because they are not interchangeable.

1 3 5 7 9 10 8 6 4 2

CONTENTS

INTRODUCTION

The Mediterranean conjures up as many vibrant colours as there are countries in the region. Azure skies, white-gold sands, bright, whitewashed walls, brilliant reds, greens, yellows, purples and oranges are seen in abundance throughout the fifteen countries that surround this beautiful sea. A quick tour will take us from the shores of Spain, to France, Italy, Greece, Turkey, Syria, Lebanon, Israel, and into Africa to Egypt, Libya, Tunisia, Algeria and Morocco. And then to the islands of Malta and Cyprus which are truly Mediterranean, encircled by the sea. Although very different, all these countries share a similar terrain and climate, as well as the sea, and this is perfectly reflected in the essence of the food that is loved by all.

There are some basic ingredients that are used throughout the region, and these have strong historical links. In ancient times, the area surrounding the Mediterranean Sea was colonized for various periods by the Phoenicians, Greeks and Romans, who shared a basic cultivation of wheat, olives and grapes. These, in turn, became bread, oil and wine – three components that are still very important in the Mediterranean diet today. With the building of ships came import and export,

and spices and flavourings, such as saffron, cloves and allspice, were introduced through North Africa and Arabia. These are still popular all over the Mediterranean, appearing in both sweet and savoury dishes. Nuts, too, are an ingredient common to many of the countries. Almonds, pistachios and pine nuts are perhaps the most frequently used.

Fresh fish and seafood have been traditionally dominant in regional dishes. The Mediterranean has hundreds of different species of fish and crustacea that are marketed locally and beyond. Visit a large fish market in any part of the region and you will be amazed by the fantastic variety of fish, many of which are completely unknown, except to the locals and fishermen. Although the Mediterranean Sea is tiny in relation to other seas and oceans, and suffers from the effects of pollution and low food supplies, some of the most delectable dishes of these countries still rely upon fresh fish.

Perhaps the most characteristic ingredient, however, is olive oil, which varies in flavour from region to region. Italy, France and Spain produce some of the best, and extra virgin olive oil gives the finest flavour of all, while a mixture of peanut oil and olive oil will produce a lighter dressing. Recent research proves this diet to be a very healthy one. Olive oil, used in cooking, contains a high proportion of mono-unsaturated fats.

A Greek salad and a bowl of olives (right).

Vegetables are the key element to the flavours of the winter time. Pumpkins, Jerusalem artichokes, tomatoes, spinach, peppers and asparagus are just a few of the many varieties of vegetables used to make soups. These, eaten with plenty of bread, provide a filling and nourishing meal on a cold day. Many soups are created using simple recipes, containing pulses such as lentils and chick-peas, or meat for a more hearty meal. There are special feast-day soups, and soups to eat after sunset during the fast of Ramadan.

However, the most characteristic Mediterranean soups are based on vegetables, pulses and, of course, fish and seafood. Fish stew and soups are typically Mediterranean and a varied mixture of fish, such as monkfish, bass, bream and red mullet, can be combined with aromatic flavourings such as saffron, herbs, garlic and orange peel to make an intensely flavoured fish stock.

The climate of these Mediterranean countries has ensured that salads and cold dishes have always been very popular. There are plenty of wonderful and, of course, fresh ingredients that are cleverly combined to produce

Fresh figs (above) are enjoyed during the summer, while a glass of local wine (left) is delicious with any meal.

delicious results. In its simplest form, a salad in France, Spain or Italy consists of lettuce dressed with a vinaigrette, often to be eaten after the main course or before the cheese is served. In addition, there are composed salads, with specific ingredients and a special dressing, that are complete dishes in their own right. These include all sorts of foodstuffs, such as olives or goat's cheese.

Desserts also make good use of the abundance of fresh produce. For a special occasion a colourful selection of seasonal fruits such as figs, plums, apricots, peaches, melons and cherries makes a stunning finale. Alternatively, there are many cooked, sweet desserts that can be enjoyed after a meal

or as a snack in the afternoon. These delicacies, such as Halva and Baklava, make use of many of the spices that originally were introduced from the Far East. Traditionally, the ingredients and cooking methods of these sweet dishes served as a means of preservation in the hot weather. Today, they continue to provide a burst of energy on a warm, sunny afternoon.

Meat recipes do not feature so strongly in the region's cuisine. The countryside around the Mediterranean can be quite harsh with no lush fields for animals to graze. Beasts are often slaughtered young, with baby lamb and goat being favourite meats, while cattle are a rare sight. Many rural families used to keep a pig that was slaughtered and the meat preserved to feed them through the chilly winter months. This has inspired the wonderful dried sausages and cured hams which are still popular today all over the world.

Poultry and game have always played an important role in Mediterranean cooking. This is largely due to the dry, rugged and, in some places, mountainous land which does not provide good pasture for cattle. Ducks, and in particular chickens, are more popular and accessible to the poorer people of the region, who often raise them on their own land. Chicken is a versatile ingredient because, whilst having its own characteristic taste,

it also absorbs other flavours easily. It is often cooked with fresh, dried or preserved fruits, or nuts and spices.

Grains and pulses are very popular, with wheat being the oldest and most dominant cereal grown in the region. Although wheat is the chief staple ingredient, centuries of trading have intermingled dishes that were originally associated with one country, such as pasta and couscous. Rice has been central to Mediterranean cookery for over twelve thousand years.

Perhaps Mediterranean food is best described as "peasant food", not in a derogatory sense, but as a homage to the people who have provided us with such a vast and wonderful repertoire of recipes, ancient and new. There is an inspiring array of dishes to choose from that are intricately prepared and flavoursome as well as extremely simple and subtle. Whatever your tastes, bring the shores of the Mediterranean into your home with this impressive collection of enjoyable and delicious dishes.

Lemons preserved in salt, with herbs and spices, can add a subtle, fragrant taste to many dishes – remember to rinse off the salt before use.

Soups and Starters

Soups are an important feature in the cuisines of the Mediterranean. Some have become famous worldwide, such as Italy's satisfying mixed vegetable soup, minestrone, or the deep-red chilled fresh tomato soup, gazpacho, from Spain. Many are meals in themselves, needing little accompaniment other than a sprinkling of freshly grated parmesan cheese and some crusty French bread, or a country-style loaf such as Italian ciabatta.

For starters, choose from the classic Italian pairing of prosciutto with fresh figs which is always popular; the dips and spreads of Greece – hummus and taramasalata; the Spanish favourites, chorizo in red wine, and spinach empanadillas; and the French red onion galettes and camembert fritters.

MINESTRONE WITH PESTO

Originally from Italy, but a favourite worldwide, minestrone is a substantial mixed vegetable soup made with almost any combination of fresh seasonal vegetables. Short pasta or rice, or pesto sauce, may also be added.

INGREDIENTS
1.5 litres/2½ pints/6¼ cups stock or water,
or a combination of both
45ml/3 tbsp olive oil
1 large onion, finely chopped
1 leek, sliced
2 carrots, finely chopped
1 celery stick, finely chopped
2 garlic cloves, finely chopped
2 potatoes, peeled and cut into small dice
1 bay leaf
1 sprig fresh thyme, or 1.5ml/¼ tsp
dried thyme
115g/4oz/¾ cup peas, fresh or frozen
2–3 courgettes, finely chopped
3 tomatoes, peeled and finely chopped
425g/15oz/2 cups cooked or canned
beans, such as cannellini
45ml/3 tbsp pesto sauce
freshly grated Parmesan cheese, to serve
salt and ground black pepper

SERVES 6

1 In a large saucepan, heat the stock or water until it reaches simmering point.

2 In another saucepan heat the olive oil. Stir in the onion and leek, and cook for 5–6 minutes, or until the onion softens.

3 Add the carrots, celery and garlic, and cook over a moderate heat, stirring often, for a further 5 minutes. Add the potatoes and cook for a further 2–3 minutes.

4 Pour in the hot stock or water, and stir well. Add the bay leaf and thyme and season with salt and pepper. Bring to the boil, then reduce the heat slightly, and leave to cook for 10–12 minutes more.

5 Stir in the peas, if fresh, and the finely chopped courgettes and simmer for a further 5 minutes. Add the frozen peas, if using, and the chopped tomatoes. Cover the pan, bring slowly to the boil, then simmer the mixture for about 5–8 minutes.

6 About 20 minutes before serving the minestrone, remove the lid, and stir in the beans. Simmer for 10 minutes. Stir in the pesto sauce. Taste and adjust the seasoning if necessary. Simmer for a further 5 minutes, then remove the pan from the heat. Allow the soup to stand for a few minutes, to bring out the flavours, then serve in warmed bowls. Serve the grated Parmesan separately.

EGG AND CHEESE SOUP

I n this classic Roman soup, eggs and cheese are beaten into hot stock, producing a slightly "curdled" texture characteristic of the dish.

INGREDIENTS
3 eggs
45ml/3 tbsp fine semolina
90ml/6 tbsp freshly grated
Parmesan cheese
pinch of nutmeg
1.5 litres/2¹/₂ pints/6¹/₄ cups cold meat or
chicken stock
salt and ground black pepper
12 rounds of French bread, to serve

SERVES 6

COOK'S TIP
To avoid the soup curdling too much, don't allow the stock to start boiling after you have added the egg mixture.

1 Break the eggs into a bowl, then add the semolina and Parmesan cheese and beat together with a fork or wire whisk. Stir in the nutmeg. Beat in 250ml/8fl oz/1 cup of the meat or chicken stock. Set aside.

2 Meanwhile, pour the remaining stock into a large saucepan and heat gently for a few minutes, stirring occasionally, until the stock reaches simmering point.

3 When the stock is hot, a few minutes before you are ready to serve the soup, whisk the egg mixture into the stock. Raise the heat slightly, and bring it barely to the boil. Season with the salt and pepper. Cook for 3–4 minutes. As the egg cooks, the soup will not be completely smooth.

4 To serve, toast the rounds of French bread on both sides and place two in each soup bowl. Ladle the hot soup over the bread and serve immediately.

ONION SOUP

Recipes for onion soup vary around the world, but this is the absolute classic – once the morning pick-me-up for workers at Les Halles, the food market in central Paris.

INGREDIENTS
30ml/2 tbsp butter
15ml/1 tbsp oil
3 large onions, thinly sliced
5ml/1 tsp soft brown sugar
15ml/1 tbsp flour
2 × 275g/10oz cans condensed
beef consommé
30ml/2 tbsp medium sherry
10ml/2 tsp Worcestershire sauce
8 slices French bread
15ml/1 tbsp wholegrain mustard
115g/4oz/1 cup Gruyère cheese, grated
salt and ground black pepper
chopped fresh parsley, to garnish

SERVES 4

1 Heat the butter and oil in a large pan and add the onions and brown sugar. Cook gently for about 20 minutes, stirring occasionally, until the onions start to turn golden brown.

2 Stir in the flour and cook for a further 2 minutes. Pour in the consommé, plus two cans of water, then add the sherry and Worcestershire sauce. Season well, cover, and simmer gently for 25–30 minutes.

VARIATION
Omit the mustard and, instead, rub the croûtes on each side with the cut side of a garlic clove before adding the Gruyère cheese.

3 Preheat the grill and, just before serving, toast the bread lightly on both sides. Spread one side of each slice with the mustard and top with the grated cheese. Grill the toasts until bubbling and golden.

4 Ladle the soup into soup plates. Place two croûtes on top of each plate of soup and garnish with chopped fresh parsley. Serve at once.

GAZPACHO

This classic Spanish no-cook soup is ideal for taking on picnics as it can be packed straight from the fridge. Keep the chopped vegetables in separate bowls and hand them round for people to help themselves.

INGREDIENTS
1 slice white bread, crusts removed
1 garlic clove
30ml/2 tbsp extra virgin olive oil
30ml/2 tbsp white wine vinegar
6 large ripe tomatoes, skinned and finely chopped
1 small onion, finely chopped
2.5ml/½ tsp paprika
pinch of ground cumin
150ml/¼ pint/⅔ cup tomato juice
salt and ground black pepper

To Garnish
1 green pepper, seeded and chopped
½ cucumber, peeled, seeded and chopped

For the Croutons
2 slices bread, cubed and deep fried

SERVES 6

1 Soak the slice of bread in enough cold water just to cover and leave for about 5 minutes, then mash with a fork.

2 Pound the garlic, oil and vinegar using a pestle and mortar, or purée in a blender or food processor. Then stir this mixture into the bread.

3 Spoon the mixture into a large bowl and stir in the tomatoes, onion, spices and tomato juice. Season, then chill. Make the garnishes and croûtons.

4 To serve, ladle the soup into six chilled soup plates and then hand round the garnishes and croûtons separately.

PASTA AND LENTIL SOUP

The small brown lentils which are grown in central Italy are usually used for this wholesome soup, but green lentils are equally suitable and may be substituted, if preferred.

INGREDIENTS
*225g/8oz/1 cup dried green or
brown lentils
90ml/6 tbsp olive oil
50g/2oz/¼ cup diced ham or salt pork
1 onion, finely chopped
1 celery stick, finely chopped
1 carrot, finely chopped
2 litres/3½ pints/8 cups chicken stock or
water, or a mixture
1 fresh sage leaf or a pinch of dried sage
1 fresh thyme sprig or
1.5ml/¼ tsp dried thyme
175g/6oz/1½ cups ditalini or other small
soup pasta
salt and ground black pepper*

SERVES 4–6

1 Pick over the lentils carefully, discarding any small stones or other pieces of grit. Place them in a bowl, add cold water to cover, and soak for 2–3 hours.

2 Heat the oil in a large saucepan. Sauté the ham for 2–3 minutes. Add the onion, and cook for 5 minutes. Stir in the celery and carrot, and cook for 5 minutes more.

3 Drain the lentils, rinse them well, then drain again. Add them to the pan, stirring thoroughly to coat them in the fat. Pour in the stock or water, with the herbs, and bring the soup to the boil. Cook over a medium heat for about 1 hour or until the lentils are tender.

4 Stir in the pasta and cook until just tender. Season with salt and pepper to taste. Allow the soup to stand for a few minutes before serving in heated bowls.

GALICIAN BROTH

T his delicious main course soup is a speciality of Galicia, in the far north-west of Spain. It is a very warming, chunky meat and vegetable broth. For extra colour, a few onion skins can be added when cooking the gammon, but remember to remove them before serving.

INGREDIENTS
450g/1lb piece gammon
2 bay leaves
2 onions, sliced
10ml/2 tsp paprika
675g/1½lb potatoes, cut into large chunks
225g/8oz spring greens
425g/15oz can haricot or cannellini beans, drained
salt and ground black pepper

SERVES 4

1 Soak the piece of gammon overnight in cold water. Drain and put in a large saucepan with the bay leaves, onions and 1.5 litres/2½ pints/6¼ cups cold water.

2 Bring to the boil then reduce the heat and simmer very gently for about 1½ hours until the meat is tender.

3 Drain the meat, reserving the cooking liquid, and leave to cool slightly. Discard the skin and any excess fat from the meat and cut into small chunks. Return to the pan with the paprika and potatoes. Cover and simmer gently for 20 minutes.

4 Cut away the tough central cores from the spring greens. Roll up the leaves and cut into thin shreds with a very sharp knife. Add to the pan with the beans and simmer for 10 minutes. Season to taste and serve the broth hot.

ALMOND SOUP

This simple and refreshing soup is of Spanish peasant origin. Unless you want to spend time pounding the ingredients by hand, a blender or food processor is essential.

INGREDIENTS
115g/4oz fresh white bread
115g/4oz/1 cup blanched almonds
2 garlic cloves, sliced
75ml/5 tbsp olive oil
25ml/1½ tbsp sherry vinegar
salt and ground black pepper
toasted flaked almonds and a few
seedless green and black grapes, skinned
and halved, to garnish

SERVES 6

1 Break the bread into a bowl and pour over 150ml/¼ pint/⅔ cup cold water. Leave for 5 minutes.

2 Process the almonds and garlic in a blender or food processor until very finely ground. Then blend in the bread.

3 Gradually add the olive oil until the mixture forms a smooth paste. Add the sherry vinegar, then 600ml/1 pint/2½ cups cold water, and process the mixture until absolutely smooth.

4 Turn into a bowl and season with salt and ground black pepper, adding a little more water if the soup is very thick. Chill for at least 2–3 hours.

5 Ladle into soup plates and scatter with toasted flaked almonds and the green and black grapes.

COOK'S TIP
This soup must be served very cold. If liked, add one or two ice cubes to each soup plate to serve.

RICE AND BROAD BEAN SOUP

This thick Italian soup makes the most of fresh broad beans while they are in season. It works well with frozen beans for the rest of the year.

INGREDIENTS

1kg/2¼lb broad beans in their pods, or
400g/14oz shelled broad beans,
thawed if frozen
90ml/6 tbsp olive oil
1 onion, finely chopped
2 tomatoes, peeled and finely chopped
225g/8oz/1 cup risotto rice
25g/1oz/2 tbsp butter
1 litre/1¾ pints/4 cups boiling chicken
stock or water
salt and ground black pepper
freshly grated Parmesan cheese,
to serve (optional)

SERVES 4

1 Shell the beans if they are fresh. Bring a large saucepan of water to the boil, add the fresh or frozen beans and blanch them for 3–4 minutes. Drain the beans, rinse under cold water, then drain again. Squeeze the beans between finger and thumb to pop them out of their skins.

2 Heat the oil in a large saucepan. Add the onion and cook over a low heat for 5 minutes until it softens. Stir in the beans, and cook for about 5 minutes, stirring often to coat them with the oil. Season with salt and pepper. Add the tomatoes and cook for 5 minutes more, stirring often.

3 Stir in the rice and cook for 1–2 minutes, then add the butter, stirring until it melts. Pour in the stock or water, a little at a time. Continue cooking the soup until the rice is tender. Taste for seasoning and adjust if necessary. Serve hot, with grated Parmesan, if using.

FISH SOUP

This hearty soup is typically Tuscan; served over toasted French bread or ciabatta, it is a meal in itself.

INGREDIENTS

1kg/2¼lb mixed whole fish or fish fillets
(such as coley, dogfish, whiting, red
mullet or cod)
90ml/6 tbsp olive oil, plus extra to serve
1 onion, finely chopped
1 celery stick, chopped
1 carrot, chopped
60ml/4 tbsp chopped fresh parsley
175ml/6fl oz/¾ cup dry white wine
3 tomatoes, peeled and chopped
2 garlic cloves, finely chopped
1.5 litres/2½ pints/6 cups hot fish stock
or water
salt and ground black pepper
rounds of French bread, to serve

SERVES 6

1 Scale and clean any whole fish, discarding all innards, but leaving the heads on. Cut the fillets into large pieces. Rinse in cold water, and pat dry with kitchen paper. Heat the oil in a large pan and cook the onion over a low heat for 5 minutes. Stir in the celery and carrot, and cook for 5 minutes more. Add the parsley.

2 Pour in the wine, raise the heat, and cook until the liquid has reduced by half. Stir in the tomatoes and garlic. Cook for 3–4 minutes, stirring occasionally. Pour in the stock or water, and bring to the boil. Cook over a medium heat for 15 minutes.

3 Stir in the fish. Simmer for 10–15 minutes, or until it is tender. Season with salt and pepper. Remove the fish from the soup with a slotted spoon. Discard any skin or bones, then purée the flesh in a food processor or pass through a food mill.

4 Stir the fish purée into the saucepan, until well combined. Heat the soup to simmering point. Toast the bread, and drizzle lightly with olive oil. Place two or three pieces of bread in each heated soup bowl, then pour on the soup.

COOK'S TIP
If the soup is cooked until it reduces to the consistency of a sauce, it makes an excellent topping for pasta.

RED ONION GALETTES

To give these French pastries a sharp edge, scatter some chopped anchovies over before baking.

INGREDIENTS
60–75ml/4–5 tbsp olive oil
500g/1¼lb red onions, sliced
1 garlic clove, crushed
30ml/2 tbsp chopped fresh mixed herbs,
such as thyme, parsley and basil
225g/8oz ready-made puff pastry
15ml/1 tbsp sun-dried tomato paste
ground black pepper
thyme sprigs, to garnish

SERVES 4

1 Heat 30ml/2 tbsp of the oil in a pan and add the onions and garlic. Cook, covered, for 15–20 minutes, stirring occasionally, until soft but not browned. Stir in the herbs.

2 Preheat the oven to 220°C/425°F/Gas 7. Divide the pastry into four equal pieces and roll out each one to a 15cm/6in round on a lightly floured surface.

3 Flute the edges by crimping them with your fingers *(left)*. Prick all over with a fork. Place the rounds on baking sheets and chill them for 10 minutes.

4 Mix 15ml/1 tbsp of the remaining olive oil with the sun-dried tomato paste and brush over the centres of the rounds, leaving a 1cm/½in border. Spread the onion mixture over the pastry rounds and grind over plenty of pepper. Drizzle over a little more oil, then bake for about 15 minutes, until the pastry is crisp and golden. Serve hot, garnished with thyme sprigs.

POTATO CAKES WITH GOAT'S CHEESE

Crispy potato cakes form the base of this melt-in-your-mouth starter. The goat's cheese and green salad transform it from the French peasant dish it was originally to *haute cuisine*.

INGREDIENTS

450g/1lb potatoes, coarsely grated
10ml/2 tsp chopped fresh thyme
1 garlic clove, crushed
2 spring onions, finely chopped
30ml/2 tbsp olive oil
50g/2oz/4 tbsp unsalted butter
2 × 65g/2½oz Crottins de Chavignol (firm goat's cheeses)
salt and ground black pepper
thyme sprigs, to garnish
mixed green salad, to serve

SERVES 2–4

1 Using your hands, squeeze out the moisture from the potatoes, then carefully combine with the chopped thyme, garlic, spring onions and seasoning.

2 Heat half the oil and butter in a non-stick frying pan. Add two large spoonfuls of the potato mixture and press firmly down with a spoon. Cook for 3–4 minutes on each side until golden.

3 Drain the potato cakes on kitchen paper and keep warm. Make two more potato cakes in the same way with the remaining mixture. Meanwhile, preheat the grill.

4 Cut the cheeses in half horizontally. Place one half cheese, cut-side up, on each potato cake *(right)*. Grill for 2–3 minutes until golden. Garnish with thyme sprigs and serve at once with the salad.

GARLIC PRAWNS

I n Spain, *Gambas al Ajillo* are traditionally cooked in small earthenware dishes, but a frying pan serves just as well.

INGREDIENTS

60ml/4 tbsp olive oil
2–3 garlic cloves, finely chopped
16 cooked whole Mediterranean prawns
15ml/1 tbsp chopped fresh parsley
lemon wedges and French bread, to serve

SERVES 4

1 Heat the oil in a large frying pan and add the garlic. Stir-fry for 1 minute, until the garlic begins to turn brown.

2 Add the Mediterranean prawns and stir-fry for 3–4 minutes, coating them well with the flavoured oil.

3 Add the parsley, remove from the heat and serve four prawns per person in heated bowls, with the flavoured oil spooned over them. Serve with lemon wedges for squeezing and French bread to mop up the delicious juices.

MEDITERRANEAN GARLIC TOASTS

T hese garlic toasts are served as a starter in Spain. With a topping of plum tomatoes, mozzarella cheese and salami, they also make a filling snack.

INGREDIENTS
150g/5oz mozzarella cheese, drained
2 plum tomatoes
½ French loaf
1 garlic clove, halved
30ml/2 tbsp olive oil, plus extra
for brushing
12 small salami slices
15ml/1 tbsp fresh torn basil, or 5ml/1 tsp
dried basil
salt and ground black pepper
fresh basil sprigs, to garnish

SERVES 4

1 Preheat a moderate grill. Cut the mozzarella cheese into 12 slices and each tomato into six slices. Cut the French bread in half and slice each half horizontally.

2 Place the bread under the grill, cut-side up, and toast lightly. While the bread is still warm, rub the cut sides of the garlic on each cut side of the bread, then drizzle over about 7.5ml/½ tbsp of the olive oil.

3 Top each toast with three slices of salami, three slices of mozzarella and three slices of tomato. Brush the tops with a little more olive oil (*left*), season well and sprinkle over the fresh or dried basil.

4 Return to the grill and toast for about 3 minutes, until the cheese has melted. Remove and serve hot, garnished with sprigs of fresh basil.

AUBERGINE DIP

This is a delicious velvet-textured dip that can be simply spread on slices of bread, or eaten as an accompaniment to more strongly flavoured dishes. It is called *melitzanasalata*.

INGREDIENTS
1 large aubergine
1 small onion
2 garlic cloves
30ml/2 tbsp olive oil
45ml/3 tbsp chopped fresh parsley
75ml/5 tbsp crème fraîche
red Tabasco sauce, to taste
juice of 1 lemon, to taste
salt and freshly ground black pepper
crusty white bread or toast, to serve

SERVES 4

COOK'S TIP
The aubergine can be roasted in the oven at 200°C/400°F/Gas 6 for about 20 minutes, if preferred.

---

1 Preheat the grill. Place the whole aubergine on a baking sheet and grill it for 20–30 minutes, turning occasionally, until the skin is blackened and wrinkled, and the aubergine feels soft when squeezed.

2 Cover the aubergine with a clean dish towel and leave to cool for 5 minutes.

3 Finely chop the onion and garlic. Heat the oil in a frying pan and cook the onion and garlic for 5 minutes until softened but not browned.

4 Peel the skin from the aubergine. Mash the flesh into a pulpy purée.

5 Stir in the onion mixture, parsley and crème fraîche. Add Tabasco, lemon juice and seasoning. Serve on toast or crusty white bread with a garnish of your choice.

DATES WITH CHORIZO

A delicious combination of fresh dates and spicy chorizo sausage is used for this Spanish tapas dish. Serve with a glass of fino sherry.

INGREDIENTS
50g/2oz chorizo sausage
12 fresh dates, stoned
6 rashers streaky bacon
oil, for frying
plain flour, for dusting
1 egg, beaten
50g/2oz/1 cup fresh breadcrumbs

SERVES 4–6

1 Trim the ends of the chorizo sausage, and peel away the skin. Cut into 2cm/¾in slices. Cut these in half lengthways, then in half again, giving 12 pieces.

2 Stuff each date with a piece of chorizo, closing the date around it. Stretch the bacon rashers, by running the back of a knife along the edge of the rasher, then cut each in half widthways. Wrap a piece of bacon around each date. Secure with a wooden cocktail stick.

3 Heat the oil in a deep pan; it should be at least 1cm/½in deep. Dust the dates with flour, then dip in the beaten egg, and finally coat in breadcrumbs. Fry in the hot oil, turning them, until golden. Remove with a slotted spoon and drain on kitchen paper. Serve immediately.

SPINACH EMPANADILLAS

T hese little pastry turnovers are filled with ingredients that illustrate the strong Moorish influence on Spanish cuisine – pine nuts and raisins.

INGREDIENTS
25g/1oz/3 tbsp raisins
25ml/1½ tbsp olive oil
*450g/1lb fresh spinach, washed
and chopped*
*6 canned anchovies, drained and
finely chopped*
2 garlic cloves, finely chopped
25g/1oz/¼ cup pine nuts, chopped
350g/12oz ready-made puff pastry
1 egg, beaten
salt and ground black pepper

MAKES 20

1 To make the filling, soak the raisins in warm water for 10 minutes. Drain and roughly chop. Heat the oil in a large sauté pan or wok, add the spinach, stir, then cover and cook over a low heat for 2 minutes. Uncover, increase the heat and let any liquid evaporate. Add the seasoning, anchovies and garlic, and cook, stirring, for a further 1 minute. Remove from the heat, add the raisins and pine nuts, and leave to cool.

2 Preheat the oven to 180°C/350°F/Gas 4. Roll out the pastry on a floured surface to 3mm/⅛in thick. Using a 7.5cm/3in round pastry cutter, cut out 20 circles. Place 10ml/2 tsp filling in the middle of each circle, then brush the edges with water. Bring up the sides of the pastry and seal *(left)*. Press the edges with a fork. Place on a greased baking sheet, brush with the egg and bake for about 15 minutes, until golden. Serve warm.

TAPAS OF ALMONDS, OLIVES AND CHEESE

apas are small savoury snacks, enjoyed all over Spain, often accompanied by a glass of wine.

INGREDIENTS
FOR THE MARINATED OLIVES
2.5ml/½ tsp coriander seeds
2.5ml/½ tsp fennel seeds
5ml/1 tsp chopped fresh rosemary
10ml/2 tsp chopped fresh parsley
2 garlic cloves, crushed
15ml/1 tbsp sherry vinegar
30ml/2 tbsp olive oil
115g/4oz/⅔ cup each black and green olives

FOR THE MARINATED CHEESE
150g/5oz goat's cheese
90ml/6 tbsp olive oil
15ml/1 tbsp white wine vinegar
5ml/1 tsp black peppercorns
1 garlic clove, sliced
3 sprigs fresh tarragon or thyme

FOR THE SALTED ALMONDS
1.5ml/¼ tsp cayenne pepper
30ml/2 tbsp sea salt
25g/1oz butter
60ml/4 tbsp olive oil
200g/7oz/1¼ cups blanched almonds

SERVES 6–8

1 For the marinated olives, crush the coriander and fennel seeds using a pestle and mortar. Mix together with the herbs, garlic, vinegar and oil and pour over the olives in a small bowl. Cover and chill in the fridge for up to 1 week.

2 For the marinated cheese, cut the cheese into bite-size pieces, leaving the rind on. Place in a small bowl. Mix together the oil, wine vinegar, peppercorns, garlic and sprigs of tarragon or thyme. Pour over the cheese Cover the bowl and chill in the fridge for up to 3 days.

3 For the salted almonds, mix together the cayenne pepper and sea salt in a bowl. Melt the butter with the olive oil in a frying pan. Add the almonds and fry quite gently, stirring, for about 5 minutes, or until the almonds are evenly golden all over.

4 Add to the salt mixture and toss together until the almonds are coated. Leave to cool, then store in a jar or airtight container for up to 1 week.

5 To serve the tapas, arrange in small, shallow serving dishes. Use fresh sprigs of tarragon to garnish the cheese and sprinkle the almonds with sea salt, if liked.

COOK'S TIP
If serving with pre-dinner drinks, provide cocktail sticks for spearing the olives and cheese.

SPANISH OMELETTE

Spanish omelette belongs in every cook's repertoire and can vary according to what you have in store. This version includes soft white beans and is finished with a layer of toasted sesame seeds.

INGREDIENTS
30ml/2 tbsp olive oil
5ml/1 tsp sesame oil
1 Spanish onion, chopped
1 small red pepper, seeded and diced
2 celery sticks, chopped
400g/14oz can soft white beans, drained
8 eggs
45ml/3 tbsp sesame seeds
salt and ground black pepper
green salad, to serve

SERVES 4

VARIATION
You can also use sliced cooked potatoes, any seasonal vegetables, baby artichoke hearts and chick-peas in a Spanish omelette.

1 Heat the olive oil and sesame oil in a 30cm/12in paella pan or frying pan. Add the onion, pepper and celery and cook until softened but not coloured.

2 Add the drained soft white beans to the pan, stir to combine, and cook gently over a low heat until the mixture is heated through.

3 In a large bowl, beat the eggs with a fork until well combined, season well with salt and ground black pepper and pour over the ingredients in the pan.

4 Stir in the egg mixture with a flat wooden spoon until it just begins to stiffen, then allow to firm over a low heat for about 6–8 minutes. Remove from the heat.

5 Preheat a moderate grill. Sprinkle the omelette with the sesame seeds and brown evenly under the grill. Watch to ensure that the seeds do not burn.

6 Cut the omelette into thick wedges and serve warm with a green salad. It is also delicious served cold.

DOLMADES

T he exact ingredients of this traditional Greek dish vary from region to region. Vine leaves and cooked rice are essential, however.

INGREDIENTS
250g/9oz fresh vine leaves
30ml/2 tbsp olive oil
1 large onion, finely chopped
250g/9oz minced lamb
75g/3oz/½ cup cooked rice
30ml/2 tbsp chopped fresh parsley
30ml/2 tbsp chopped fresh mint
30ml/2 tbsp snipped fresh chives
3–4 spring onions, finely chopped
juice of 2 lemons
30ml/2 tbsp tomato purée (optional)
30ml/2 tbsp sugar
salt and freshly ground black pepper
yogurt and pitta bread, to serve (optional)

SERVES 4–6

1 Blanch the vine leaves in boiling water for 1–2 minutes to soften them.

2 Heat the olive oil in a large frying pan and fry the onion for a few minutes until slightly softened. Add the lamb and fry over a moderate heat until well browned, stirring frequently. Season with salt and pepper.

3 Stir the cooked rice, chopped herbs, spring onions and the juice of one of the lemons into the lamb. Add the tomato purée, if using, and then knead the mixture with your hands until thoroughly blended.

4 Place a vine leaf on a chopping board with the vein side up. Place 15ml/1 tbsp of the lamb mixture on the vine leaf and fold the stem end over the meat. Fold the sides in towards the centre and then fold over to make a neat parcel. Continue until all the filling has been used up.

5 Line the base of a large saucepan with several unstuffed leaves and arrange the rolled leaves in tight layers on top. Stir the remaining lemon juice and the sugar into about 150ml/¼ pint/⅔ cup water and pour over the leaves. Place a heat resistant plate over the dolmades to keep them in shape. Cover the pan tightly and cook over a very low heat for 2 hours, checking occasionally and adding a little extra water should the pan begin to boil dry. Serve warm or cold with yogurt and warm pitta bread, if liked.

COOK'S TIP
If using preserved vine leaves, soak them overnight in cold water and then rinse several times before use.

HUMMUS

This Greek chick-pea and sesame seed dip is good with crackers, warm pitta bread or raw vegetables. The tahini – sesame seed paste – is available from delicatessens and health food stores. Try to make twice the quantity if you can, as hummus freezes well.

INGREDIENTS
225g/8oz/1¼ cups chick-peas,
soaked overnight
115g/4oz/½ cup tahini paste
2 garlic cloves, crushed
juice of 1–2 lemons
60ml/4 tbsp olive oil
salt
cayenne pepper and flat leaf parsley,
to garnish
pitta bread, to serve

SERVES 4

COOK'S TIP
You can use a can (400g/14oz) of chick-peas in this recipe as the final result will be just as good. Simply omit the soaking and boiling and just drain, reserving the liquid for use later. Season carefully if extra salt has been added to the can.

1 Drain the chick-peas and cook them in fresh boiling water for 10 minutes. Reduce the heat and simmer for about 1 hour or until soft. Drain the chick-peas, reserving the cooking liquid.

2 Put the chick-peas into a food processor or blender and add the tahini paste, garlic and a little lemon juice. Process until smooth. Season and add enough cooking liquid to process until creamy. Add more lemon juice or liquid as the hummus stiffens after resting.

3 Spoon the hummus on to plates, swirl it with a knife and drizzle with olive oil. Sprinkle with cayenne pepper, garnish with parsley and serve with pitta bread.

TARAMASALATA

This delicious speciality makes an excellent starter to any meal. It is perhaps one of the most famous Greek dips.

INGREDIENTS
115g/4oz smoked mullet roe
2 garlic cloves, crushed
30ml/2 tbsp grated onion
60ml/4 tbsp olive oil
4 slices white bread, crusts removed
juice of 2 lemons
30ml/2 tbsp milk or water
freshly ground black pepper
warm pitta bread, to serve

SERVES 4

1 Place the smoked roe, garlic, onion, oil, bread and lemon juice in a blender or food processor and process until smooth.

2 Add the milk or water and process again for a few seconds. (This will give the taramasalata a creamier texture.)

3 Pour the taramasalata into a serving bowl, cover with clear film and chill for 1–2 hours before serving. Sprinkle the dip with freshly ground black pepper and serve with warm pitta bread.

COOK'S TIP
Since the roe of grey mullet is expensive, smoked cod's roe is often used instead for this dish. It is paler than the burnt-orange colour of mullet roe but is still very good.

39

CHORIZO IN RED WINE

This simple Spanish tapas dish is flamed just before serving. If you like, use small chorizo sausages and leave them whole. Provide cocktail sticks for your guests to spear the sausages when you serve this dish.

INGREDIENTS
225g/8oz cured chorizo sausage
90ml/6 tbsp red wine
30ml/2 tbsp brandy
chopped fresh parsley, to garnish

SERVES 4

COOK'S TIP
After cooking, the chorizo sausage can be cooled, then chilled for up to 24 hours before using.

1 Prick the chorizo sausage(s) in several places with a fork and place them in a saucepan with the red wine. Bring to the boil, lower the heat, then cover and simmer gently for 15 minutes. Remove from the heat and leave the sausage(s) to cool in the covered pan for 2 hours.

2 Remove the chorizo sausage(s) from the pan and reserve the wine.

3 Using a sharp knife, cut the chorizo sausage(s) into 1cm/½in slices.

4 Heat the chorizo slices in a heavy-based frying pan, then pour over the brandy and light it very carefully with a match. When the flames have died down, add the reserved wine and cook for 2–3 minutes until it is piping hot. Serve garnished with chopped parsley.

PROSCIUTTO WITH FIGS

T he hams cured in the region of Parma in northern Italy are held to be the finest in the country. Prosciutto makes an excellent starter when sliced paper-thin and served with fresh figs.

INGREDIENTS
12 paper-thin slices prosciutto
8 ripe green or black figs
crusty bread and unsalted butter, to serve

SERVES 4

1 Separate the slices of prosciutto and arrange them decoratively, in a spiral pattern, on a large serving platter.

2 Wipe the figs with a damp cloth. Cut them almost into quarters but do not cut all the way through the base. If the skins are tender, they may be eaten along with the inner fruit.

3 Arrange the quartered figs on top of the slices of prosciutto. Serve immediately with a basket of crusty country bread and pats of unsalted butter. Alternatively, serve with grissini, the Italian bread sticks, or warmed ciabatta rolls.

CARPACCIO WITH ROCKET

C arpaccio is a fine Italian dish of raw beef marinated in lemon juice and olive oil. It is traditionally served with flakes of fresh Parmesan cheese. Use very fresh meat of the best quality.

INGREDIENTS

1 garlic clove, halved
1½ lemons
50ml/2fl oz/¼ cup extra virgin olive oil
2 bunches rocket
4 very thin slices of beef top round
salt and ground black pepper
115g/4oz/1 cup Parmesan cheese, thinly shaved, to serve

SERVES 4

1 Rub a small bowl all over with the cut side of the garlic. Squeeze the lemon juice into the bowl. Whisk in the olive oil and season with salt and pepper. Allow to stand for at least 15 minutes before using.

2 Carefully wash the rocket and tear off any thick stalks. Spin the leaves in a salad spinner or pat dry. Arrange the rocket around the edge of a serving platter, or divide among four individual plates.

3 Place the beef in the centre of the platter, and pour on the dressing, spreading it evenly over the meat. Arrange the shaved Parmesan on top of the meat slices and serve at once.

CAMEMBERT FRITTERS

T hese deep-fried cheeses are a French speciality, simple to prepare. They are served with a red onion marmalade which can be made in advance and stored in the fridge.

INGREDIENTS
8 individual portions of Camembert
1 egg, beaten
115g/4oz/1 cup dried breadcrumbs, to coat
oil, for deep-frying
parsley sprigs, to garnish

FOR THE MARMALADE
45ml/3 tbsp sunflower oil
45ml/3 tbsp olive oil
900g/2lb red onions, sliced
15ml/1 tbsp coriander seeds, crushed
2 bay leaves
45ml/3 tbsp granulated sugar
90ml/6 tbsp red wine vinegar
10ml/2 tsp salt

SERVES 4

1 To make the marmalade, heat the oils in a large saucepan and gently fry the onions, covered, for 20 minutes or until soft. Add the remaining ingredients, stir well, and cook, uncovered, for 10–15 minutes until most of the liquid is absorbed. Leave to cool.

2 To prepare the cheese, scratch the rinds lightly with a fork. Dip first in egg and then in breadcrumbs to coat well. Dip and coat a second time if necessary. Set aside.

3 Pour oil into a deep-fat fryer to one-third full and heat to 190°C/375°F/Gas 5. Add the cheeses a few at a time and fry for about 2 minutes until golden. Drain on kitchen paper and fry the rest of the cheeses, reheating the oil in between. Serve hot with the marmalade. Garnish with parsley sprigs.

COOK'S TIP
You could make these fritters with fingers of firm Brie, or try using small rounds of goat's cheese.

GOLDEN CHEESE PUFFS

S erve these French deep-fried puffs – known as *aigrettes* – with a fruity chutney and a green salad. Smaller, bite-size, ones make an excellent party snack.

INGREDIENTS
50g/2oz/½ cup plain flour
15g/½oz/1 tbsp butter
1 egg, plus 1 egg yolk, beaten
115g/4oz/1 cup finely grated mature Cheddar cheese
15ml/1 tbsp grated Parmesan cheese
2.5ml/½ tsp mustard powder
pinch of cayenne pepper
oil, for frying
salt and ground black pepper
mango chutney and salad, to serve

SERVES 4

1 Sift the flour on to a square of greaseproof paper and set aside. Place the butter and 150ml/¼ pint/⅔ cup water in a pan and heat until the butter is melted.

2 Bring the liquid to the boil and quickly tip in the flour all at once. Remove the pan from the heat and stir well with a wooden spoon until the mixture begins to leave the sides of the pan and forms a ball. Allow the mixture to cool slightly.

3 Gradually add the egg to the mixture, beating well after each addition. Stir in the cheeses, mustard, cayenne, and season.

4 Heat the oil in a large saucepan or deep-fat frier to 190°C/375°F/Gas 5 or until a cube of bread browns in 30 seconds. Drop four spoonfuls of the cheese mixture at a time into the hot oil and deep-fry for 2–3 minutes until golden. Using a slotted spoon, lift out the cheese puffs and leave them to drain on kitchen paper. Keep them hot in the oven while cooking the remaining mixture. Allow two puffs per person and serve immediately with a generous spoonful of mango chutney and a green salad.

Salads and Vegetables

The rich variety of salad and vegetable dishes in this chapter reflects an abundance of fresh produce. Simple salad ingredients are combined with the slightly more unusual to produce imaginative light meals and side dishes. Try, for example, broad beans mixed with Greek feta cheese; the mild bitterness of green leafy rocket combined with the sweetness of pears; the Cypriot classic of fried halloumi cheese on top of a mixed green salad with sweet, juicy grapes.

Nothing combines the vegetables of the Mediterranean better than the classic ratatouille, but simple vegetable dishes, such as lightly cooked broccoli flavoured with garlic, are just as typical of Mediterranean cooking.

MARINATED GOAT'S CHEESE WITH HERBS

The marinated cheeses in this French recipe are also delicious spread on toasted French bread, brushed with olive oil and rubbed with garlic.

INGREDIENTS
4 fresh soft goat's cheeses, halved
90ml/6 tbsp chopped fresh mixed parsley,
thyme and oregano
2 garlic cloves, chopped
12 black peppercorns, lightly crushed
150ml/¼ pint/⅔ cup extra virgin olive oil
salad leaves, to serve

SERVES 4–8

COOK'S TIP
Any herbs can be added to the marinade – try chervil, tarragon, chives and basil. If you prefer, reserve the herb-flavoured oil, and use it to make a salad dressing.

---

1 Arrange the individual fresh goat's cheeses in a single layer in a large, shallow non-metallic dish.

2 Put the chopped herbs, garlic and crushed peppercorns in a blender or food processor. Start the machine, then pour in the oil and process until the mixture is fairly smooth.

3 Spoon the herb mixture over the cheeses, then cover and leave to marinate in the fridge for 24 hours, basting the cheeses occasionally.

4 Remove the cheeses from the fridge about 30 minutes before serving and allow them to come to room temperature.

5 Serve the cheeses on a bed of salad leaves and spoon over a little of the olive oil and herb mixture.

VARIATION
For a subtle flavour and an attractive colour contrast, use pink peppercorns instead of black.

BROAD BEAN AND FETA SALAD

This recipe is loosely based on a typical medley of fresh-tasting Greek salad ingredients – broad beans, tomatoes and feta cheese. It is lovely when served warm or cold as a starter or main course accompaniment.

INGREDIENTS
900g/2lb broad beans, shelled, or
350g/12oz shelled frozen beans
60ml/4 tbsp olive oil
175g/6oz plum tomatoes, halved, or
quartered if large
4 garlic cloves, crushed
115g/4oz/1 cup firm feta cheese, cut
into chunks
45ml/3 tbsp chopped fresh dill
12 black olives
salt and freshly ground black pepper
chopped fresh dill, to garnish

SERVES 4–6

1 Cook the fresh or frozen broad beans in boiling, salted water until just tender. Drain and set aside.

2 Meanwhile, heat the oil in a heavy-based frying pan and add the tomatoes and garlic. Cook until the tomatoes are beginning to colour.

3 Add the feta cheese to the pan and toss the ingredients together for 1 minute. Mix with the drained beans, dill, olives and salt and pepper. Serve garnished with chopped dill.

GREEK SALAD

This classic salad, called *horiatiki*, is a wonderful combination of textures and flavours. The saltiness of the feta cheese is perfectly balanced by the variety of refreshing salad vegetables.

INGREDIENTS
1 cos lettuce heart
1 green pepper
1 red pepper
½ cucumber
4 tomatoes
1 red onion
225g/8oz/1 cup feta cheese, crumbled
black olives, to garnish

FOR THE DRESSING
45ml/3 tbsp olive oil
45ml/3 tbsp lemon juice
1 garlic clove, crushed
15ml/1 tbsp chopped fresh parsley
15ml/1 tbsp chopped fresh mint
salt and freshly ground black pepper

SERVES 4

1 Chop the lettuce into bite-size pieces. Seed the peppers, remove the cores and cut the flesh into thin strips. Chop the cucumber and slice or chop the tomatoes. Cut the onion in half, then slice finely.

2 Place the chopped lettuce, peppers, cucumber, tomatoes and onion in a large bowl. Scatter the feta over the top and toss together lightly.

3 To make the dressing for the salad, blend together the olive oil, lemon juice and garlic in a small bowl. Stir in the fresh parsley and mint and season with plenty of salt and pepper to taste.

4 Carefully pour the dressing over the salad and toss together lightly. Serve the salad in its bowl, garnished with a handful of black olives.

ROCKET AND PEAR SALAD

1 Peel and core the pears and slice thickly lengthways. Moisten the flesh with lemon juice to keep it white.

2 Combine the nut oil with the pears. Add the rocket leaves and toss.

3 Turn the salad out on to four small plates and top with shavings of Parmesan cheese. Season with freshly ground black pepper and serve with the bread.

F or a sophisticated start to an elaborate meal, try this simple Italian salad of honey-rich pears, fresh Parmesan shavings and aromatic leaves of rocket. Enjoy it with a young Beaujolais or a lightly chilled Lambrusco wine.

INGREDIENTS

3 ripe pears, Williams or Packhams
10ml/2 tsp lemon juice
45ml/3 tbsp hazelnut or walnut oil
115g/4oz rocket, washed and dried
75g/3oz Parmesan cheese, shaved
ground black pepper
open-textured bread, to serve

SERVES 4

COOK'S TIP
Rocket is fairly easy to find in supermarkets, but if you have a garden, then you can grow your own from early spring to late summer.

BRESAOLA AND ONION SALAD

Bresaola is an Italian speciality. It is raw beef which has been salted in much the same way as *prosciutto di Parma*. In this salad, it is combined with sweet, juicy onions.

INGREDIENTS
2 medium onions, peeled
75–90ml/5–6 tbsp olive oil
juice of 1 lemon
12 thin slices bresaola
75g/3oz rocket, washed and dried
salt and ground black pepper

SERVES 4

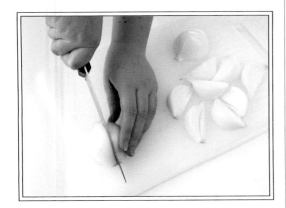

1 Slice each onion into eight wedges through the root. Arrange the wedges in a single layer in a flameproof dish. Brush them with a little of the olive oil and season well with salt and black pepper to taste.

2 Place the onion wedges under a hot grill and cook for about 8–10 minutes, turning once, until they are just beginning to soften and turn golden brown at the edges.

3 Meanwhile, to make the dressing, mix together the lemon juice and 60ml/4 tbsp of the olive oil. Add salt and black pepper to taste and whisk until thoroughly blended.

4 Pour the lemon dressing over the hot onions, mix well to coat the onions and leave until cold.

5 When the onions are cold, divide the bresaola slices among four individual serving plates and arrange the onions and rocket on top. Spoon over any remaining dressing and serve the salad immediately.

HALLOUMI AND GRAPE SALAD

F irm salty halloumi cheese is often served fried for breakfast or supper in Cyprus, where it originated from. In this recipe it is tossed with sweet, juicy grapes which really complement its distinctive flavour.

INGREDIENTS
150g/5oz mixed green salad leaves
75g/3oz seedless green grapes
75g/3oz seedless black grapes
250g/9oz halloumi cheese
45ml/3 tbsp olive oil
fresh young thyme leaves or dill,
to garnish

FOR THE DRESSING
60ml/4 tbsp olive oil
15ml/1 tbsp lemon juice
2.5ml/½ tsp caster sugar
15ml/1 tbsp chopped fresh thyme or dill
salt and freshly ground black pepper

SERVES 4

1 To make the dressing, mix together the olive oil, lemon juice and sugar. Season. Stir in the thyme or dill and set aside.

2 Toss together the salad leaves and the green and black grapes, then transfer to a large serving plate.

> COOK'S TIP
> Most large supermarkets sell ready-mixed bags of prepared salad leaves, which are ideal for use in this recipe. Experiment with various combinations to find the lettuce flavours that you like best.

3 Thinly slice the cheese. Heat the oil in a large frying pan. Add the cheese and fry briefly until turning golden on the underside. Turn the cheese with a fish slice and cook the other side.

4 Arrange the cheese over the salad. Pour over the dressing and garnish with thyme or dill.

SALADE NIÇOISE

s its name suggests, this famous salad is typical of the cuisine of the Nice area of southern France.

INGREDIENTS
675g/1½lb potatoes, peeled
225g/8oz French beans, trimmed
3 eggs, hard-boiled
1 cos lettuce
120ml/4fl oz/½ cup French dressing, see box below
225g/8oz small plum tomatoes, quartered
400g/14oz canned tuna in oil, drained
25g/1oz canned anchovy fillets
30ml/2 tbsp capers
12 black olives
salt and ground black pepper
basil leaves, to garnish (optional)

SERVES 4

COOK'S TIP
To make the French dressing, put 25ml/1½ tbsp white wine vinegar, 30ml/2 tbsp olive oil, 5ml/1 tsp Dijon mustard and 30ml/2 tbsp chopped, fresh mixed herbs in a screw-top jar, add salt and ground black pepper to taste and shake together.

1 Bring the potatoes to the boil in salted water and cook for 20 minutes. Boil the French beans for 6 minutes. Drain the potatoes and beans under cold running water and leave to cool.

2 Slice the potatoes thickly, and shell and quarter the eggs. Wash the lettuce and dry in a salad spinner or on a clean dish towel, then chop the leaves roughly. Put the lettuce into a large salad bowl and toss with half of the dressing.

3 Put the cooled potatoes, whole French beans and quartered tomatoes into a bowl and toss with the remaining French dressing, then arrange them decoratively over the bed of salad leaves in the salad bowl.

4 Break up the tuna fish into large flakes with a fork and distribute over the salad with the anchovy fillets, capers, and olives. Season to taste with salt and pepper and serve immediately. If you like, garnish with basil leaves.

SPINACH SALAD WITH BACON AND PRAWNS

S erve this warm salad as it is served in France, with plenty of crusty bread for mopping up the delicious juices. It tastes every bit as good as it looks.

INGREDIENTS
105ml/7 tbsp olive oil
30ml/2 tbsp sherry vinegar
2 garlic cloves, finely chopped
5ml/1 tsp Dijon mustard
12 cooked unshelled king prawns
115g/4oz streaky bacon, rinded and cut into strips
about 115g/4oz fresh young spinach leaves
½ head oak-leaf lettuce, roughly torn
salt and ground black pepper

SERVES 4

1 To make the dressing, whisk together 90ml/6 tbsp of the olive oil with the vinegar, garlic, mustard and seasoning in a small pan. Heat gently until thickened slightly, then keep warm.

2 Carefully pull off the heads, then remove the shells and legs from the prawns, leaving the tails intact. Set aside.

3 Heat the remaining oil in a frying pan and fry the bacon until golden and crisp, stirring occasionally. Add the prawns and stir-fry for a few minutes until warmed through.

4 Meanwhile, arrange the spinach and torn oak-leaf lettuce leaves on four individual serving plates.

5 Spoon the bacon and prawns on to the salad leaves, then pour over the hot dressing. Serve at once.

BROCCOLI WITH OIL AND GARLIC

This is a very simple way of transforming steamed or blanched broccoli into a succulent Mediterranean dish. Peeling the broccoli stalks is easy, and allows for even cooking.

INGREDIENTS
1kg/2¼lb fresh broccoli
90ml/6 tbsp extra virgin olive oil
2–3 garlic cloves, finely chopped
salt and ground black pepper

SERVES 6

1 Wash the broccoli. Using a small sharp knife, cut off any woody parts at the base of the broccoli, then peel the stems. Cut any very long or wide stalks in half.

2 Boil some water in the bottom of a saucepan equipped with a steamer, or bring a large saucepan of water to the boil. If steaming the broccoli, put it in the steamer and cover tightly. Cook for 8–12 minutes or until the stems are just tender when pierced with the point of a knife. Remove from the heat. If blanching, drop the broccoli into the pan of boiling water and cook for 5–6 minutes, until just tender. Drain.

3 In a frying pan large enough to hold all the broccoli pieces, gently heat the oil with the garlic. When the garlic is light golden (do not let it brown or it will be bitter) add the broccoli, and cook over moderate heat for 3–4 minutes, turning carefully to coat it with the hot oil. Tip into a serving bowl and season with salt and pepper. Serve hot or cold.

AVOCADO, TOMATO AND MOZZARELLA PASTA SALAD

A stylish, summer salad made from ingredients representing the three colours of the Italian flag – a sunny cheerful dish!

INGREDIENTS
175g/6oz pasta bows (farfalle)
6 ripe red tomatoes
225g/8oz mozzarella
1 large ripe avocado
30ml/2 tbsp pine nuts, toasted
1 fresh basil sprig, to garnish

FOR THE DRESSING
90ml/6 tbsp olive oil
30ml/2 tbsp wine vinegar
5ml/1 tsp balsamic vinegar (optional)
5ml/1 tsp wholegrain mustard
pinch of sugar
salt and ground black pepper
30ml/2 tbsp chopped fresh basil

SERVES 4

1 Cook the pasta in plenty of boiling salted water according to the manufacturer's instructions. Drain well and cool.

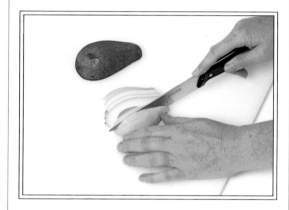

2 Slice the tomatoes and mozzarella into thin rounds. Halve the avocado, remove the stone, and peel off the skin. Slice the flesh lengthways.

3 Whisk together all the dressing ingredients, except the chopped fresh basil, in a small bowl.

4 Just before you are ready to serve the salad, arrange alternate slices of tomato, mozzarella and avocado in a spiral pattern, just slightly overlapping one another, around the edge of a large serving platter.

5 Toss the pasta with half the dressing and the chopped basil. Pile into the centre of the platter. Pour over the remaining dressing, scatter over the pine nuts and garnish the pasta with a sprig of fresh basil. Serve immediately.

> ### COOK'S TIP
> To ripen avocados, put them into a paper bag with an apple or potato and leave in a warm place for 2–3 days.

FRENCH GOAT'S CHEESE SALAD

H ere is the French salad and cheese course all on one plate. You could serve it as a quick and satisfying starter or a light lunch. The tangy flavour of goat's cheese contrasts wonderfully with the mild salad leaves.

INGREDIENTS
*200g/7oz bag prepared mixed
salad leaves
4 rashers back bacon
115g/4oz full fat goat's cheese
16 thin slices crusty white bread*

FOR THE DRESSING
*60ml/4 tbsp olive oil
15ml/1 tbsp tarragon vinegar
10ml/2 tsp walnut oil
5ml/1 tsp Dijon mustard
5ml/1 tsp wholegrain mustard*

SERVES 4

1 Preheat the grill to a medium heat. Rinse and dry the salad leaves, then arrange them in four individual bowls. Place the ingredients for the dressing in a screw-topped jar, shake together well and reserve.

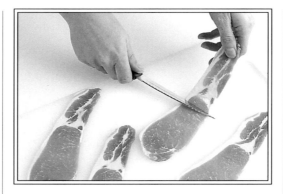

2 Lay the bacon rashers on a board, then stretch them with the back of a knife and cut each one into four. Roll each piece up and grill for 2–3 minutes.

3 Slice the goat's cheese into eight and halve each slice. Top each slice of bread with a piece of goat's cheese and place under the grill. Turn over the bacon and continue cooking with the toasts until the cheese is golden and bubbling.

4 Arrange the bacon rolls and toasts on top of the prepared salad leaves, shake the dressing well and pour a little dressing over each one.

COOK'S TIP
If you prefer, just slice the goat's cheese and place it on toasted crusty white bread. Or use wholemeal toast for a deliciously nutty flavour. Vegetarians can replace the bacon rolls with halved cherry tomatoes, for an alternative juicy flavour.

ROASTED PEPPERS WITH TOMATOES AND ARTICHOKES

This is a Sicilian-style salad, using some typical ingredients from the Italian island. The flavour improves if the salad is made two hours early.

INGREDIENTS
1 red pepper
1 yellow pepper
1 green pepper
4 sun-dried tomatoes in oil, drained
4 ripe plum tomatoes, sliced
2 cans artichokes, drained and chopped
15ml/1 tbsp capers, drained
15ml/1 tbsp pine nuts
1 garlic clove, very thinly sliced

FOR THE DRESSING
75ml/5 tbsp extra virgin olive oil
15ml/1 tbsp balsamic vinegar
5ml/1 tsp lemon juice
chopped fresh mixed herbs
salt and freshly ground black pepper

SERVES 4

1 Cut the peppers in half and remove the seeds and stalks. Cut into quarters and cook, skin-side up, under a hot grill until the skin chars. Transfer to a bowl and cover with a plate. Leave to cool then peel them (*right*) and cut into strips.

2 Thinly slice the sun-dried tomatoes. Arrange the peppers and fresh tomatoes on a serving dish and scatter over the artichokes, sun-dried tomatoes, capers, pine nuts and garlic.

3 To make the dressing, mix together the olive oil, balsamic vinegar, lemon juice and chopped herbs and season with salt and pepper to taste. Pour over the salad just before serving.

CLASSIC POTATO TORTILLA

A traditional Spanish tortilla contains potatoes and onions. Whilst other ingredients can be added to the basic egg mixture, it is generally accepted that this classic tortilla is one that cannot be improved upon.

INGREDIENTS
450g/1lb small waxy potatoes, peeled
1 Spanish onion
45ml/3 tbsp vegetable oil
4 eggs
salt and freshly ground black pepper
flat leaf parsley, to garnish

SERVES 6

1 Cut the potatoes into thin slices and the onion into rings.

2 Heat about 30ml/2 tbsp of the oil in a 20cm/8in heavy-based frying pan. Add the sliced potatoes and the onion rings and cook over a low heat for about 10 minutes until the potatoes are just tender. Remove from the heat.

3 In a large mixing bowl, beat together the eggs with a little salt and freshly ground black pepper. Stir in the cooked sliced potatoes and onion rings.

4 Heat the remaining oil in the frying pan and pour in the potato and egg mixture. Cook very gently for 5–8 minutes until the mixture is almost set.

5 Place a large plate upside-down over the pan, invert the tortilla on to the plate and then slide it back into the pan. Cook for 2–3 minutes more until the underside of the tortilla is golden brown. Cut into wedges and serve, garnished with flat leaf parsley.

BAKED FENNEL

F ennel is widely eaten all over Italy, both in its raw and cooked form. It is delicious married with the sharpness of Parmesan cheese in this dish.

INGREDIENTS
1kg/2¼lb fennel bulbs, washed and
halved
50g/2oz/4 tbsp butter
40g/1½oz/⅓ cup freshly grated
Parmesan cheese

SERVES 4–6

VARIATION
For a more substantial version of this dish, scatter 75g/3oz chopped ham, bacon or pancetta over the fennel before topping with the grated Parmesan cheese.

1 Preheat the oven to 200°C/400°F/Gas 6. Cook the fennel in a large pan of boiling water until soft but not mushy. Drain.

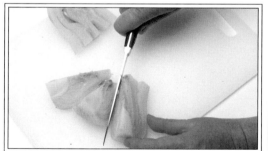

2 Cut the fennel bulbs lengthways into four or six pieces. Place them in a buttered baking dish.

3 Dot with butter, then sprinkle with the grated Parmesan. Bake for 20 minutes until golden brown. Serve at once.

AUBERGINE BAKED WITH CHEESE

T his famous dish is a speciality of Italy's southern regions. In Campania, around Naples, slices of hard-boiled egg are sometimes added with the mozzarella.

INGREDIENTS
1kg/2¼lb aubergines
flour, for coating
oil, for frying
40g/1½oz/⅓ cup freshly grated
Parmesan cheese
400g/14oz/2 cups mozzarella, sliced
very thinly
salt and ground black pepper

FOR THE TOMATO SAUCE
60ml/4 tbsp olive oil
1 onion, very finely chopped
1 garlic clove, finely chopped
450g/1lb tomatoes, fresh or canned,
chopped, with their juice
a few fresh basil leaves or parsley sprigs
salt and ground black pepper

SERVES 4–6

1 Cut the aubergines into rounds about 1cm/½in thick, sprinkle with salt, and leave to drain for about 1 hour.

2 Meanwhile make the tomato sauce. Heat the oil in a saucepan. Add the onion and cook over a moderate heat for 5–8 minutes until translucent. Stir in the garlic and the tomatoes (add 45ml/3 tbsp water if using fresh tomatoes). Add the herbs and season. Cook for 20–30 minutes. Purée in a blender.

3 Pat the aubergine slices dry with kitchen paper. Coat lightly in flour. Heat a little oil in a large frying pan. Add one layer of aubergine, and cook, covered, over a low heat, turning once, until soft. Repeat with the remaining slices.

4 Preheat the oven to 180°C/350°F/Gas 4. Grease a wide shallow baking dish. Pour a little tomato sauce in the base. Cover with a layer of aubergine. Sprinkle with a little Parmesan, season and cover with a layer of mozzarella and some sauce. Repeat, finishing with tomato sauce and a sprinkling of Parmesan. Sprinkle with a little olive oil, and bake for 45 minutes.

GRILLED POLENTA WITH GORGONZOLA

Grilled polenta is delicious, and is a good way of using up cold polenta. Try it with any soft flavourful cheese. Plain grilled polenta is also a good accompaniment to stews and soups.

INGREDIENTS
1.5 litres/2½ pints/6¼ cups water
15ml/1 tbsp salt
350g/12oz/2½ cups polenta flour
225g/8oz/1¼ cups grated Gorgonzola or
other cheese, at room temperature

SERVES 6–8 AS A SNACK
OR APPETIZER

1 Bring the water to the boil in a large heavy-based saucepan, and add the salt. Reduce the heat to a simmer, and gradually add the polenta flour in a fine rain. Stir constantly with a whisk until all the polenta has been added.

2 Switch to a long-handled wooden spoon, and continue to stir the polenta over a low to moderate heat until it is a thick mass, and pulls away from the sides of the pan. This may take from around 25–50 minutes, depending on the type of flour used. For best results, never stop stirring the polenta until you remove it from the heat.

3 When the polenta is cooked, sprinkle a work surface or large board with a little water. Spread the polenta out onto the surface in a layer approximately 1.5cm/¾in in thickness. Allow to cool completely. Preheat the grill.

4 Cut the polenta into triangles. Grill the pieces until hot and speckled with brown on both sides. Spread with the Gorgonzola or other cheese. Serve immediately as a starter, a snack or as an accompaniment.

POTATO AND RED PEPPER FRITTATA

F resh herbs make all the difference in this Italian-style omelette – fresh parsley or chives could be substituted for the chopped mint.

INGREDIENTS
450g/1lb small new potatoes
6 eggs
30ml/2 tbsp chopped fresh mint
30ml/2 tbsp olive oil
1 onion, chopped
2 garlic cloves, crushed
2 red peppers, seeded and roughly chopped
salt and ground black pepper
mint sprigs, to garnish

SERVES 3–4

1 Cook the potatoes in boiling salted water until just tender. Drain, leave to cool slightly, then cut into thick slices.

2 Whisk together the eggs, mint and seasoning in a bowl, then set aside. Heat the oil in a large frying pan.

3 Add the onion, garlic, peppers and potatoes to the pan and cook, stirring, for 5 minutes.

4 Pour the egg mixture over the vegetables and stir gently. Push the mixture into the centre of the pan *(left)* as it cooks to allow the liquid egg to run on to the base. Turn the heat to low.

5 Once the egg mixture is lightly set, place the pan under a hot grill for 2–3 minutes, until golden brown. Serve the frittata hot or cold, cut into wedges and garnished with mint sprigs.

GLOBE ARTICHOKES WITH BEANS AND AIOLI

A s with the French *aioli,* there are many recipes for the Spanish equivalent. The one used here is exceptionally garlicky, a perfect partner to freshly cooked vegetables.

INGREDIENTS
FOR THE AIOLI
6 large garlic cloves, sliced
10ml/2 tsp white wine vinegar
250ml/8fl oz/1 cup olive oil
salt and ground black pepper

FOR THE SALAD
225g/8oz French beans
3 small globe artichokes
15ml/1 tbsp olive oil
pared rind of 1 lemon
coarse salt and ground black pepper,
to sprinkle
lemon wedges, to garnish

SERVES 4

COOK'S TIP
To eat artichokes, the leaves should be pulled from the base and used to scoop a little sauce. It is the fleshy end of the leaf that is eaten. The base and heart of the artichoke can also be eaten.

---

1 To make the *aioli,* put the garlic and vinegar in a blender or mini food processor. With the machine running, gradually pour in the olive oil until the mixture is thickened and very smooth. (Alternatively, crush the garlic to a paste with the vinegar and gradually beat in the oil using a hand whisk.) Season to taste.

2 To make the salad, cook the beans in boiling water for 1–2 minutes until slightly softened. Drain.

3 Trim the artichoke stalks close to the base. Cook the artichokes in a large pan of boiling salted water for about 30 minutes or until you can easily pull away a leaf from the base. Drain well.

4 Halve the cooked artichokes lengthways with a sharp knife and carefully pull out the choke using a teaspoon.

5 Arrange the artichokes and beans on serving plates and drizzle with the oil. Scatter with the pared lemon rind and season with coarse salt and pepper. Spoon the *aioli* into the artichoke hearts and serve warm, garnished with lemon wedges.

VARIATION
Mediterranean baby artichokes are sometimes available and, unlike the larger ones, can be eaten whole. Cook until just tender, then simply cut in half to serve.

Canned artichoke hearts, thoroughly drained and sliced, may be substituted when fresh ones are not available.

TABBOULEH

This classic Lebanese salad is very popular in many Mediterranean countries. It makes an ideal substitute for a rice dish on a buffet table and is also excellent with cold sliced lamb.

INGREDIENTS
175g/6oz/1 cup fine bulgur wheat
juice of 1 lemon
45ml/3 tbsp olive oil
60ml/4 tbsp fresh parsley, finely chopped
45ml/3 tbsp fresh mint, chopped
4–5 spring onions, chopped
1 green pepper, seeded and sliced
salt and freshly ground black pepper
2 large tomatoes, diced, and
black olives, to garnish

SERVES 4

1 Put the bulgur wheat in a bowl. Add enough cold water to cover the wheat and let it stand for at least 30 minutes and up to 2 hours.

2 Drain the bulgur wheat and squeeze it with your hands to remove any excess water. (The wheat will swell to double the size.) Spread it out on kitchen paper to allow the wheat to dry completely.

3 Place the bulgur wheat in a large mixing bowl, add the lemon juice, olive oil and a little salt and pepper to taste. Allow the mixture to stand for 1–2 hours, if possible, in order for all the flavours in the salad to develop fully.

4 Add the chopped parsley, mint, spring onions and pepper and mix well. Garnish with diced tomatoes and olives and serve.

RATATOUILLE

A highly versatile vegetable stew from Provence, ratatouille is delicious hot or cold, on its own or with eggs, pasta, fish or meat – particularly roast lamb.

INGREDIENTS
2 large aubergines, roughly chopped
4 courgettes, roughly chopped
150ml/¼ pint/⅔ cup olive oil
2 onions, sliced
2 garlic cloves, chopped
1 large red pepper, seeded and roughly chopped
2 large yellow peppers, seeded and roughly chopped
fresh rosemary sprig
fresh thyme sprig
5ml/1 tsp coriander seeds, crushed
3 plum tomatoes, skinned, seeded and chopped
8 basil leaves, torn
salt and freshly ground black pepper
fresh parsley or basil sprigs, to garnish

SERVES 4

1 Sprinkle the aubergines and courgettes with salt, then place in a colander with a plate and a weight on top to extract the bitter juices. Leave to stand for 30 minutes.

2 Heat the olive oil in a large pan. Add the onions, fry for 6–7 minutes, until soft, then add the garlic and cook for 2 minutes.

3 Rinse the aubergines and courgettes and pat dry. Add to the saucepan with the peppers, increase the heat and sauté until the peppers are just turning brown.

4 Add the herbs and coriander seeds, then cover the pan and cook the vegetables gently for about 40 minutes.

5 Add the tomatoes and season well. Cook gently for a further 10 minutes, until the vegetables are soft but not too mushy. Remove the sprigs of herbs. Stir in the torn basil leaves and adjust the seasoning. Serve the dish warm or cold, garnished with sprigs of fresh parsley or basil.

STUFFED TOMATOES AND PEPPERS

Colourful peppers and tomatoes make perfect containers for various meat and vegetable stuffings. This rice and herb version uses a variety of typically Greek ingredients.

INGREDIENTS
2 large ripe tomatoes
1 green pepper
1 yellow or orange pepper
60ml/4 tbsp olive oil, plus extra
for sprinkling
2 onions, chopped
2 garlic cloves, crushed
50g/2oz/½ cup blanched
almonds, chopped
75g/3oz/scant ½ cup long grain rice,
boiled and drained
15g/½oz fresh mint, roughly chopped
15g/½oz fresh parsley, roughly chopped
25g/1oz/2 tbsp sultanas
45ml/3 tbsp ground almonds
salt and freshly ground black pepper
chopped fresh herbs, to garnish

SERVES 4

1 Preheat the oven to 190°C/375°F/Gas 5. Cut the tomatoes in half and scoop out the pulp and seeds using a teaspoon. Leave the tomatoes to drain on kitchen paper with cut sides down. Roughly chop the tomato pulp and seeds.

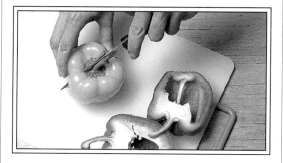

2 Halve the peppers, leaving the cores intact, and scoop out the seeds. Brush the peppers with 15ml/1 tbsp of the olive oil and bake on a baking tray for 15 minutes. Place the pepper and tomato cases in a shallow ovenproof dish and season with salt and pepper.

3 Fry the onions in the remaining oil for 5 minutes. Add the garlic and chopped almonds and fry for 1 minute more.

4 Remove the pan from the heat and stir in the rice, chopped tomatoes, mint, parsley and sultanas. Season well with salt and pepper and spoon the mixture into the tomato and pepper cases.

5 Pour 150ml/¼ pint/⅔ cup boiling water around the tomatoes and peppers and bake, uncovered, in the preheated oven for 20 minutes. Scatter with the ground almonds and sprinkle with a little extra oil. Return to the oven and bake for a further 20 minutes, or until turning golden. Serve garnished with fresh herbs.

VARIATION
Small aubergines or large courgettes also make good vegetables for stuffing. Halve and scoop out the centres of the vegetables, then oil the vegetable cases and bake for about 15 minutes. Chop the centres, fry for 2–3 minutes to soften and add to the stuffing mixture. Fill the aubergine or courgette cases with the stuffing and bake as for the peppers and tomatoes.

SAUTÉED PEAS WITH HAM

W hen fresh peas are in season in Florence, they are stewed with a little ham and onion and served as a substantial side dish.

INGREDIENTS
45ml/3 tbsp extra virgin olive oil
115g/4oz/½ cup diced pancetta or
rindless smoked streaky bacon
45ml/3 tbsp finely chopped onion
1kg/2¼lb peas in the pod (about
300g/11oz shelled) or 275g/10oz frozen
petits pois, thawed
30–45ml/2–3 tbsp water
few mint leaves or parsley sprigs
salt and ground black pepper

SERVES 4

1 Heat the oil in a medium saucepan, and sauté the pancetta or bacon and onion for 2–3 minutes.

2 Stir in the shelled fresh or thawed frozen peas. Add the water. Season with salt and pepper and mix well to coat with the oil.

3 Add the fresh herbs, cover, and cook over a medium heat until tender. This may take from 5 minutes for sweet fresh peas, to 15 for tougher, older peas. Serve as a side dish with meat or omelette dishes.

MUSHROOM MEDLEY

The wonderful range of mushrooms – both fresh and dried – available in France is put to good use in this exciting side dish.

INGREDIENTS
15g/½oz packet dried ceps or porcini mushrooms (optional)
60ml/4 tbsp olive oil
225g/8oz button mushrooms, halved or sliced
115g/4oz oyster mushrooms
115g/4oz fresh shiitake mushrooms, or 25g/1oz dried and soaked mushrooms
2 garlic cloves, crushed
10ml/2 tsp ground coriander
45ml/3 tbsp chopped fresh parsley
salt and ground black pepper

SERVES 4

1 If you are using dried ceps or porcini mushrooms (and they do give a good rich flavour), soak them in a little hot water just to cover for 20 minutes.

2 In a large saucepan, heat the oil and add all the mushrooms, including the soaked ceps or porcini, if using. Stir well, cover and cook gently for 5 minutes.

3 Crush the garlic and add to the pan with the coriander and seasoning. Stir well then cook for a further 5 minutes, until the mushrooms are tender and much of the liquid has been reduced. Stir in the chopped parsley, then allow the mushrooms to cool slightly before serving.

POTATO GRATIN

This is a simpler version of the classic French *gratin dauphinois*. It is perfect for a light supper or lunch dish, or can be served as an accompaniment to a more substantial meal.

INGREDIENTS
1 garlic clove
5 large baking potatoes, peeled
45ml/3 tbsp freshly grated Parmesan cheese
600ml/1 pint/2½ cups vegetable or chicken stock
pinch of freshly grated nutmeg
salt and ground black pepper

SERVES 4

1 Preheat the oven to 200°C/400°F/Gas 6. Halve the garlic clove and rub over the base and sides of a gratin dish measuring about 20 × 30cm/8 × 12in.

2 Slice the potatoes very thinly and arrange a third of them in the dish. Sprinkle with a little grated cheese, salt and pepper. Pour over some of the stock.

3 Continue layering the potatoes and cheese as before, then pour over the rest of the stock. Sprinkle with nutmeg.

4 Bake in the oven for 1¼–1½ hours or until the potatoes are tender and the tops well browned.

COOK'S TIP
For a potato and onion gratin, slice an onion and layer with the potato.

CHICORY, CARROT AND ROCKET SALAD

A bright and colourful salad which combines two of France's most popular vegetables, chicory and rocket. If you cannot find rocket, baby spinach or watercress can be used instead.

INGREDIENTS
3 carrots, coarsely grated
about 50g/2oz fresh rocket,
roughly chopped
1 large head of chicory, separated
into leaves

FOR THE DRESSING
45ml/3 tbsp sunflower oil
15ml/1 tbsp hazelnut or walnut
oil (optional)
30ml/2 tbsp cider or white wine vinegar
10ml/2 tsp clear honey
5ml/1 tsp grated lemon rind
15ml/1 tbsp poppy seeds
salt and ground black pepper

SERVES 4–6

1 Mix together the carrots and rocket in a large bowl and season well.

2 Shake the dressing ingredients together in a screw-top jar then pour on to the carrot mixture. Toss the salad thoroughly.

3 Line shallow salad bowls with the chicory leaves and spoon the salad into the centre *(right)*. Serve lightly chilled.

AUBERGINE BAKE

The Greeks love to use aubergines in their cooking. Add some eggs and bake in the oven and you get a filling and delicious meal.

INGREDIENTS
60ml/4 tbsp oil
1 onion, finely chopped
3–4 garlic cloves, crushed
4 aubergines, cut lengthways into
quarters
6 eggs
2–3 saffron strands, soaked in
15ml/1 tbsp boiling water
5ml/1 tsp paprika
salt and freshly ground black pepper
chopped fresh parsley, to garnish
herb bread and salad, to serve

SERVES 4

1 Preheat the oven to 180°C/350°F/Gas 4. Heat 30ml/2 tbsp of the oil in a frying pan and fry the onion until golden. Add the garlic and fry for about 2 minutes, then add the aubergines and cook for 10–12 minutes until soft and golden brown. Allow to cool and then chop the aubergines.

2 Beat the eggs in a large bowl and stir in the aubergine mixture, saffron water, paprika and seasoning (*left*). Place the remaining oil in a deep ovenproof dish. Heat in the oven for a few minutes, then add the egg and aubergine mixture. Bake for about 30–40 minutes until set. Garnish with chopped fresh parsley and serve with herb bread and a salad.

TOMATO AND OKRA STEW

O kra is frequently used in the cooking of Greece and Turkey. It releases a sticky sap when cooked, which helps to thicken this stew.

INGREDIENTS
15ml/1 tbsp olive oil
1 onion, chopped
400g/14oz can pimientos, drained
2 x 400g/14oz cans chopped tomatoes
275g/10oz okra
30ml/2 tbsp chopped fresh parsley
salt and freshly ground black pepper

SERVES 4

1 Heat the oil in a saucepan. Add the onion and cook for 2–3 minutes.

2 Using a small, sharp knife, roughly chop the drained pimientos and add them to the onion in the saucepan. Add the cans of chopped tomatoes and mix everything together thoroughly.

3 Cut the tops off the okra and add them to the pan. Season, then bring to the boil. Lower the heat, cover and simmer for about 12 minutes. Stir in the chopped parsley and serve at once.

ONION TART

The Provençal version of pizza, this is a versatile dish that can be served hot or cold. It is ideal for summer picnics.

INGREDIENTS
275g/10oz packet pizza base mix
5ml/1 tsp olive oil, plus extra
for drizzling

FOR THE TOPPING
30ml/2 tbsp olive oil
6 onions, thinly sliced
2 garlic cloves, crushed
50g/2oz can anchovy fillets, sliced in
half lengthways
8 black olives, stoned
10ml/2 tsp chopped fresh thyme, or
2.5ml/½ tsp dried thyme
salt and ground black pepper

SERVES 6

1 Heat the oil in a frying pan, add the sliced onions and garlic and season lightly. Fry gently, stirring occasionally, for about 40 minutes, or until the onions are soft but not too brown.

2 Preheat the oven to 220°C/425°F/Gas 7. Empty the pizza base mix into a bowl, stir in 250ml/8fl oz/1 cup warm water and add the oil. Mix to a dough and then knead for about 5 minutes.

3 Lightly grease a 33 × 23cm/13 × 9in Swiss roll tin. Roll out the dough on a lightly floured surface to fit the tin and press into the base. Spread the cooked onions evenly over the dough and then arrange the anchovy fillets on top in a lattice pattern. Scatter over the olives and chopped thyme and drizzle with a little olive oil. Place in a large sealed plastic bag and leave to rise in a warm place for 15 minutes.

4 Bake for 10 minutes. Reduce the oven temperature to 190°C/375°F/Gas 5 and cook for 15–20 minutes or until golden brown around the edges. Serve warm or cold.

PROVENÇAL BEANS

M uch of the cuisine of Provençe is based on the tomato. Here tomatoes and garlic transform plain beans into a memorable dish.

INGREDIENTS
5ml/1 tsp olive oil
1 small onion, finely chopped
1 garlic clove, crushed
225g/8oz runner beans,
trimmed and sliced
225g/8oz French beans,
trimmed and sliced
2 tomatoes, peeled and chopped
salt and ground black pepper

SERVES 4

1 Heat the oil in a heavy-based saucepan and sauté the onion over a medium heat until softened but not browned.

2 Add the garlic and sauté for 1–2 minutes, then stir in the sliced runner beans, French beans and chopped tomatoes. Season generously with salt and pepper, (*left*), then cover the pan tightly with a lid.

3 Cook over a fairly low heat, shaking the pan occasionally, for about 30 minutes, or until the beans are tender. Serve hot.

STEWED LENTILS

 n Tuscany lentils are often eaten as an accompaniment to duck, but they are also good by themselves.

INGREDIENTS
450g/1lb/2 cups green or brown lentils
30ml/2 tbsp extra virgin olive oil
50g/2oz/¼ cup of pancetta, cut into
5cm/2in squares or diced salt pork
1 onion, very finely chopped
1 celery stick, very finely sliced
1 carrot, very finely chopped
1 garlic clove, peeled and left whole
1 bay leaf
45ml/3 tbsp chopped fresh parsley
salt and ground black pepper

SERVES 6

1 Pick over the lentils carefully, removing any stones or other particles. Place them in a large bowl and add water to cover. Soak for several hours, then drain.

2 Heat the oil in a large heavy-based saucepan. Add the pancetta or salt pork and cook for 3–4 minutes. Stir in the onion; cook over a low heat for about 5 minutes.

3 Add the celery and carrot and cook for 3–4 minutes more, stirring occasionally.

4 Tip the lentils into the pan, stirring to coat them with the fat. Pour in enough boiling water just to cover the lentils. Add the whole garlic clove, the bay leaf and the parsley, with salt and pepper to taste. Stir well. Cook over a medium heat for about 1 hour, or until the lentils are tender. Discard the garlic and bay leaf. Serve hot or at room temperature, as you prefer.

BROAD BEAN PURÉE WITH HAM

Peeled broad beans are tender and sweet. They contrast beautifully with slightly salty *prosciutto crudo* in this Tuscan combination.

INGREDIENTS

1kg/2¼lb fresh broad beans in their pods,
or 400g/14oz shelled broad beans, thawed
if frozen
1 onion, finely chopped
2 small potatoes, peeled and diced
45ml/3 tbsp extra virgin olive oil
50g/2oz/¼ cup diced prosciutto crudo
ground black pepper

SERVES 4

1 Place the shelled beans in a saucepan with water to cover. Bring to the boil and cook for 5 minutes. Drain. As soon as they are cool enough to handle, squeeze the beans between finger and thumb to pop them out of their skins.

2 Place the peeled beans in a saucepan and add the onion and potatoes. Pour in enough water just to cover the vegetables. Bring to the boil. Lower the heat slightly, cover and simmer for 15–20 minutes, until the vegetables are very soft. Check the water level occasionally.

3 Heat the oil in a small frying pan and sauté the ham until it is just golden.

4 Purée the bean mixture in a food processor, or mash it by hand. Return it to the pan. If it is too moist, cook it over a medium heat until it reduces slightly. Stir in the ham, with the oil used for cooking it (*right*). Add pepper to taste. Cook for 2 minutes and serve.

Fish and Seafood

The Mediterranean sea is a rich source of fish and seafood, and, not surprisingly, the countries that surround it base many of their dishes on the sea's produce. In general, fish is cooked simply, but may be combined with a flavoursome sauce, such as the classic Spanish Romesco.

Mussels, prawns and lobster are amongst the most popular of seafood. Again, their treatment tends to be simple, as in the combination of mussels and white wine in moules marinière. Squid is also a favourite, especially in the western Mediterranean, where it is known as calamari. Here, it is often combined with other succulent fish and shellfish, or stuffed with delicious Mediterranean ingredients.

BAKED AROMATIC SEA BASS

Sea bass is a firm white-fleshed fish which is at its best cooked in this simple Tuscan style. Use fresh herbs, if possible.

INGREDIENTS
1 large sea bass, about 1.5kg/3–3½lb
4 bay leaves
few thyme sprigs
8–10 parsley sprigs
few fennel, tarragon or basil sprigs
15ml/1 tbsp black peppercorns
135ml/9 tbsp extra virgin olive oil
plain flour, for coating
salt and ground black pepper
fresh herbs, to garnish

SERVES 4

1 Gut the fish, leaving the head on. Rinse thoroughly inside and out under cold running water. Pat dry with kitchen paper. Spread out half the herbs and peppercorns in the bottom of a large shallow platter, and lay the fish on top. Arrange the remaining herbs over the fish and in its cavity. Sprinkle with 45ml/3 tbsp of the oil. Cover lightly with foil, and chill for 2 hours.

2 Preheat the oven to 200°C/400°F/Gas 6. Remove and discard all the herbs from around the fish. Pat it dry with kitchen paper. Spread a little flour on a large plate and season the fish with salt and pepper. Using a spatula, turn the fish in the flour, shaking off the excess.

3 Heat the remaining olive oil in a flameproof dish just large enough to hold the fish comfortably. When the oil is hot, brown the fish quickly on both sides. Transfer the dish to the oven and bake for 25–40 minutes, depending on the size of the fish. The fish is cooked when the dorsal fin (in the middle of the backbone) comes out easily when pulled. Garnish with the fresh herbs and serve at once.

DEEP FRIED WHITEBAIT

A spicy coating on these fish gives this favourite Greek dish, *marides*, a crunchy bite. It can also be served as a starter.

INGREDIENTS
115g/4oz/1 cup plain flour
2.5ml/½ tsp paprika
2.5ml/½ tsp ground cayenne pepper
pinch of salt
1.1kg/2½lb whitebait, thawed
if frozen
vegetable oil, for deep frying
lemon wedges, to serve

SERVES 6

1 Mix together all the dry ingredients in a large mixing bowl.

2 Place the whitebait in the bowl with the spicy flour mixture and coat thoroughly.

3 Heat the oil in a large, heavy-based saucepan until it reaches a temperature of 190°C/375°F. Fry the whitebait in batches for 2 minutes, or until the fish is golden and crispy.

4 Drain well on absorbent kitchen paper and serve hot with lemon wedges.

DEEP FRIED PRAWNS AND SQUII

P rawns (*garides*) and squid (*calamari*) are a favourite Greek combination, but any mixture of seafood can be used in this dish.

INGREDIENTS
vegetable oil, for deep frying
600g/1lb 5oz cooked prawns, shelled and deveined
600g/1lb 5oz squid (about 12) cleaned and cut into bite-size pieces
115g/4oz/1 cup flour
lemon wedges, to serve

FOR THE BATTER
2 egg whites
30ml/2 tbsp olive oil
15ml/1 tbsp white wine vinegar
90g/3½oz/scant 1 cup flour
10ml/2 tsp baking soda
75g/3oz/⅓ cup cornflour
salt and freshly ground black pepper

SERVES 6

1 Make the batter in a large mixing bowl by beating the egg whites, olive oil and vinegar together lightly with a wire whisk. Beat in the dry ingredients and whisk until well blended. Beat in 250ml/8fl oz/1 cup water, a little at a time. Cover the bowl, and allow to stand for 15 minutes.

2 Heat the oil for deep frying in a heavy-based saucepan to about 185°C/360°F, or until a small piece of bread sizzles as soon as it is dropped in.

3 Coat the prawns and squid pieces in the flour, shaking off any excess. Dip them quickly into the batter. Fry in small batches for about 1 minute, stirring with a slotted spoon to keep the pieces from sticking to each other.

4 Remove and drain on kitchen paper. Allow the oil to come back up to the correct temperature between batches. Sprinkle lightly with salt, and serve hot with lemon wedges.

ZARZUELA

arzuela is Spanish for "light opera" or "musical comedy" and the classic fish stew of the same name should be as lively and colourful as the *Zarzuela* itself. This feast of fish includes lobster and other shellfish, but you can always vary the ingredients if you wish.

INGREDIENTS
1 cooked lobster
24 live mussels or clams
1 large monkfish tail, skinned
225g/8oz squid rings
15ml/1 tbsp plain flour
90ml/6 tbsp olive oil
12 large raw prawns
2 large mild onions, chopped
4 garlic cloves, crushed
30ml/2 tbsp brandy
450g/1lb ripe tomatoes, peeled and roughly chopped
2 bay leaves
5ml/1 tsp paprika
1 red chilli, seeded and chopped
300ml/½ pint/1¼ cups fish stock
15g/½oz/2 tbsp ground almonds
30ml/2 tbsp chopped fresh parsley
salt and ground black pepper
green salad and warm bread, to serve

SERVES 6

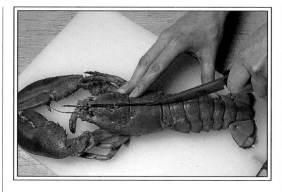

1 Using a large knife, cut the lobster in half lengthways. Remove the dark intestine. Crack the claws using a hammer.

2 Scrub the mussels or clams; discard any that are damaged or remain open when tapped. Cut the monkfish fillets from the central cartilage and cut each into three.

3 Toss the monkfish and squid rings in seasoned flour. Fry quickly in the oil on all sides. Drain and fry the raw prawns on both sides, then drain.

4 Fry the onions and two-thirds of the garlic for 3 minutes. Add the brandy and ignite with a taper. When the flames die down add the tomatoes, bay leaves, paprika, chilli and stock.

5 Bring to the boil, reduce the heat and simmer gently for 5 minutes. Add the mussels or clams, cover and cook for 3–4 minutes until the shells open.

6 Remove the mussels or clams from the sauce and discard any shells which remain closed.

7 Arrange all the fish and lobster in a large flameproof serving dish. Blend the almonds to a paste with the remaining garlic and parsley and stir into the sauce.

8 Pour the sauce over the fish and cook gently for 5 minutes until hot. Add the cooked prawns and heat through. Serve with a green salad and lots of warm bread.

COOK'S TIP
Take the serving dish to the table and ladle out the portions, making sure everyone gets a taste of all the different types of seafood.

STUFFED CALAMARI

alamari are very popular in Greece, and are quick to cook. Turn and baste them often.

INGREDIENTS

500g/1¼ lb baby squid, cleaned
1 garlic clove, crushed
3 plum tomatoes, skinned and chopped
8 sun-dried tomatoes in oil, drained and chopped
60ml/4 tbsp chopped fresh basil, plus extra to garnish
60ml/4 tbsp fresh white breadcrumbs
45ml/3 tbsp olive oil
15ml/1 tbsp red wine vinegar
salt and freshly ground black pepper
lemon juice and wedges, to serve

SERVES 4

1 Remove the tentacles from the squid and roughly chop them. Leave the main part of the squid whole.

2 Mix together the tentacles, garlic, plum tomatoes, sun-dried tomatoes, fresh basil, and breadcrumbs. Stir in 15ml/1 tbsp of the olive oil and all of the red wine vinegar. Season well with salt and pepper. Meanwhile, soak some wooden cocktail sticks in water for about 10 minutes before use to prevent them from burning.

3 With a teaspoon, fill the squid with the stuffing mixture. Secure the open ends with the cocktail sticks.

4 Brush with the remaining oil. Cook under a medium-hot grill for 4–5 minutes, turning often. Sprinkle with lemon juice and basil. Serve with lemon wedges.

FISH PLAKI

G enerally in Greece, fish is treated very simply but this recipe is a little more involved, flavouring the fish with onions, herbs and tomatoes.

INGREDIENTS

300ml/½ pint/1¼ cups olive oil
2 onions, thinly sliced
3 large well-flavoured tomatoes,
roughly chopped
3 garlic cloves, thinly sliced
5ml/1 tsp sugar
5ml/1 tsp chopped fresh dill
5ml/1 tsp chopped fresh mint
5ml/1 tsp chopped fresh celery leaves
15ml/1 tbsp chopped fresh parsley
6 cod steaks
juice of 1 lemon
salt and freshly ground black pepper
fresh dill, mint or parsley, to garnish

SERVES 6

1 Heat the oil in a large frying pan or flameproof dish. Add the onions and cook until pale golden. Add the tomatoes, garlic, sugar, dill, mint, celery leaves and parsley with 300ml/½ pint/1¼ cups water. Season with salt and pepper, then simmer, uncovered, for 25 minutes or until the liquid has reduced by a third.

2 Add the fish steaks and cook gently for 10–12 minutes or until the fish is just cooked. Remove from the heat and add the lemon juice. Cover and leave to stand for about 20 minutes before serving. Arrange the cod in a serving dish and spoon the sauce over. Garnish with herbs and serve either warm or cold.

RED MULLET WITH TOMATOES

or flavour and ease of preparation, this Greek recipe for red mullet simply cannot be beaten.

INGREDIENTS
4 red mullet, about 175–200g/6–7oz each
450g/1lb tomatoes, peeled, or
400g/14oz can plum tomatoes
60ml/4 tbsp olive oil
60ml/4 tbsp finely chopped fresh parsley
2 garlic cloves, finely chopped
120ml/4fl oz/½ cup white wine
4 thin lemon slices, cut in half
salt and freshly ground black pepper

SERVES 4

1 Scale and clean the fish without removing the liver. Wash and pat dry with kitchen paper.

2 Chop the tomatoes into small pieces. Heat the oil in a saucepan or flameproof casserole large enough to hold the fish in one layer. Add the parsley and garlic and sauté for 1 minute. Stir in the tomatoes and cook for 15–20 minutes over a moderate heat. Season with salt and pepper.

3 Add the fish to the tomato sauce and cook over a moderate to high heat for 5 minutes. Add the wine and the lemon slices. Bring the sauce back to the boil and cook for about 5 minutes more. Turn the fish over and cook for 4–5 minutes more. Remove the fish to a warmed serving platter and keep warm until needed.

VARIATION
Small sea bass may be substituted.

4 Boil the sauce for 3–4 minutes to reduce it slightly. Spoon it over the fish. Serve, decorated with the cooked lemon slices.

GRILLED SARDINES

Fresh sardines are flavoursome and firm-fleshed. They are excellent grilled and served with lemon, as they are in this simple Italian dish.

INGREDIENTS
*1kg/2lb fresh sardines, gutted and with
heads removed
olive oil, for brushing
salt and ground black pepper
45ml/3 tbsp chopped fresh parsley and
lemon wedges, to garnish*

SERVES 4–6

1 Preheat the grill. Rinse the sardines inside and out with cold running water. Pat dry thoroughly with kitchen paper.

2 Brush the sardines lightly with olive oil *(left)* and sprinkle generously with salt and pepper. Place the sardines in a single layer on the grill pan. Grill for 3–4 minutes.

3 Turn, and cook for 3–4 minutes more, or until the skins begin to brown. Serve immediately, garnished with the chopped parsley and lemon wedges.

SOLE GOUJONS WITH LIME MAYONNAISE

This simple French dish can be rustled up very quickly making an excellent light lunch or supper. If you cannot find a lime, use a lemon instead.

INGREDIENTS

200ml/7fl oz/⅞ cup good-quality mayonnaise
1 small garlic clove, crushed
10ml/2 tsp capers, rinsed and chopped
10ml/2 tsp chopped gherkins
finely grated rind of ½ lime
10ml/2 tsp lime juice
15ml/1 tbsp chopped fresh coriander
675g/1½lb sole fillets, skinned
2 eggs, beaten
115g/4oz/2 cups fresh white breadcrumbs
oil, for deep-frying
salt and ground black pepper
lime wedges, to serve

SERVES 4

1 To make the lime mayonnaise, mix together the mayonnaise, garlic, capers, gherkins, lime rind and juice and chopped coriander. Season to taste with salt and pepper. Transfer to a serving bowl and chill until required.

2 Cut the sole fillets into finger-length strips. Dip into the beaten egg, then into the breadcrumbs.

3 Heat the oil in a deep-fat fryer to 180°C/350°F/Gas 4. Add the fish in batches and fry until golden brown and crisp. Drain on kitchen paper.

4 Pile the goujons on to warmed serving plates and serve them with the lime wedges for squeezing over. Hand round the sauce separately.

HAKE WITH MUSSELS

C od and haddock cutlets will work just as well as hake in this tasty Spanish-style dish, with its delicious sauce containing both wine and sherry.

INGREDIENTS
30ml/2 tbsp olive oil
25g/1oz/2 tbsp butter
1 onion, chopped
3 garlic cloves, crushed
15ml/1 tbsp plain flour
2.5ml/½ tsp paprika
4 hake cutlets, about 175g/6oz each
225g/8oz French beans, cut into
2.5cm/1in lengths
350ml/12fl oz/1½ cups fish stock
150ml/¼ pint/⅔ cup dry white wine
30ml/2 tbsp dry sherry
16–20 live mussels, cleaned
45ml/3 tbsp chopped fresh parsley
salt and ground black pepper
crusty bread, to serve

SERVES 4

1 Heat the oil and butter in a frying pan, add the onion and cook for 5 minutes, until softened. Add the crushed garlic and cook for a further 1 minute.

2 Mix together the plain flour and paprika, then lightly dust over the hake cutlets. Push the onion and garlic mixture to one side of the frying pan, then add the hake cutlets to the pan and fry until golden on both sides.

3 Stir in the beans, fish stock, white wine and sherry, and season to taste. Bring to the boil and cook the fish over a low heat for about 2 minutes.

4 Discard any mussels that remain open when tapped. Add the mussels and parsley, cover and cook for 8 minutes, discarding any not open after cooking.

5 Serve the hake in warmed, shallow soup plates with plenty of crusty bread to mop up the juices.

FISH FILLETS WITH ORANGE AND TOMATO SAUCE

A slightly spicy and colourful sauce complements tender white fish fillets in this tasty Spanish dish.

INGREDIENTS

20g/³⁄₄oz/3 tbsp plain flour
4 fillets firm white fish such as cod, sea bass or sole, about 175g/6oz each
15g/¹⁄₂oz/1 tbsp butter or margarine
30ml/2 tbsp olive oil
1 onion, sliced
2 garlic cloves, chopped
1.5ml/¹⁄₄ tsp ground cumin
500g/1¹⁄₄lb tomatoes, peeled, seeded and chopped, or 400g/14oz can chopped tomatoes
120ml/4fl oz/¹⁄₂ cup fresh orange juice
salt and ground black pepper
orange wedges, to garnish
mange-touts, to serve

SERVES 4

1 Put the flour on a plate and season with salt and pepper. Coat the fish fillets with the flour, shaking off any excess.

2 Heat the butter or margarine and half of the oil in a large frying pan. Add the fish fillets to the pan and cook for about 3 minutes on each side until the fish is golden and the flesh flakes easily when tested.

3 When the fish is cooked, transfer to a warmed serving plate. Cover with foil and keep warm while making the sauce.

4 Heat the remaining oil in the pan. Add the onion and garlic and cook until softened, about 5 minutes.

5 Stir in the cumin, tomatoes and orange juice. Bring to the boil and cook for about 10 minutes, stirring, until thickened.

6 Garnish the fish with orange wedges and serve with mange-touts. Hand the sauce round separately.

GRILLED KING PRAWNS

Romesco sauce, from the Catalan region of Spain, is served with these prawns. It can also be used to accompany other fish and seafood.

INGREDIENTS
24 raw king prawns in the shell
30–45ml/2–3 tbsp olive oil

FOR THE ROMESCO SAUCE
2 well-flavoured tomatoes
60ml/4 tbsp olive oil
1 onion, chopped
4 garlic cloves, chopped
1 canned pimiento, drained and chopped
2.5ml/½ tsp dried chilli flakes
75ml/5 tbsp fish stock
30ml/2 tbsp dry white wine
10 blanched almonds, toasted
15ml/1 tbsp red wine vinegar
salt, to taste
lemon wedges and flat leaf parsley, to garnish

SERVES 4

1 Slash the bottoms of the tomatoes with a sharp knife. Immerse them in boiling water for 30 seconds, then refresh under cold water. Peel off the skins and roughly chop the flesh.

2 Heat 30ml/2 tbsp of the oil in a pan, add the onion and three cloves of garlic, and cook until soft. Add the chopped pimiento and tomato, with the chilli flakes, stock and wine. Cover and simmer for 30 minutes.

3 Put the almonds in a blender or food processor and grind coarsely. Add the remaining oil and garlic, and the vinegar. Process until combined. Add the tomato sauce and process until smooth.

4 Remove the heads from the prawns and, with a sharp knife, slit each one down the back and remove the black vein. Rinse under cold running water and pat dry on kitchen paper.

5 Preheat the grill. Toss the prawns in olive oil, then grill for about 2–3 minutes on each side, until pink. Arrange on a plate, garnish with lemon wedges and parsley and serve the sauce in a small bowl.

TUNA WITH PAN-FRIED TOMATOES

 n this easy-to-prepare Italian supper dish, tuna is served with a fresh, piquant sauce, olives and tomatoes.

INGREDIENTS
2 tuna steaks, about 175g/6oz each
90ml/6 tbsp olive oil
30ml/2 tbsp lemon juice
2 garlic cloves, chopped
5ml/1 tsp chopped fresh thyme
4 canned anchovy fillets, drained and finely chopped
225g/8oz plum tomatoes, halved
30ml/2 tbsp chopped fresh parsley
4–6 black olives, stoned and chopped
ground black pepper
crusty bread, to serve

SERVES 2

COOK'S TIP
If you are unable to find fresh tuna steaks, you could replace them with salmon fillets, if you like – just cook them for 1–2 minutes more on each side.

1 Place the tuna steaks in a shallow non-metallic dish. Mix 60ml/4 tbsp of the oil with the lemon juice, garlic, thyme, anchovies and pepper. Pour this mixture over the tuna and leave to marinate for at least 1 hour.

2 Lift the tuna from the marinade and place on a grill rack. Grill for 4 minutes on each side, or until the tuna feels firm to the touch, basting with some of the marinade. Take care not to overcook.

3 Meanwhile, heat the remaining oil in a frying pan. Add the tomatoes and fry for just 2 minutes on each side.

4 Divide the tomatoes equally between two warmed serving plates and scatter over the chopped parsley and olives. Place the tuna steaks on top of the tomatoes.

5 Add the remaining marinade to the pan juices and warm through. Pour over the tomatoes and tuna steaks and serve at once with crusty bread for mopping up the juices.

MEDITERRANEAN BAKED FISH

This fish bake, *Poisson au Souquet*, is said to have originated with the fishermen on the Côte d'Azur who would cook the remains of their catch for lunch in the still-warm baker's oven.

INGREDIENTS

3 potatoes
2 onions, halved and sliced
30ml/2 tbsp olive oil, plus extra
for drizzling
2 garlic cloves, very finely chopped
675g/1½ lb thick skinless fish fillets,
such as turbot or sea bass
1 bay leaf
1 thyme sprig
3 tomatoes, peeled and thinly sliced
30ml/2 tbsp orange juice
60ml/4 tbsp dry white wine
2.5ml/½ tsp saffron strands, steeped in
60ml/4 tbsp boiling water
salt and freshly ground black pepper

SERVES 4

1 Cook the potatoes in boiling salted water for 15 minutes, then drain. When the potatoes are cool enough to handle, peel off the skins and slice them thinly.

2 Meanwhile, in a heavy-based frying pan, fry the onions in the oil over a medium-low heat for about 10 minutes, stirring frequently. Add the garlic and continue cooking for a few minutes until the onions are soft and golden.

3 Preheat the oven to 190°C/375°F/Gas 5. Layer half of the cooked potato slices in a 2 litre/3⅓ pint/8 cup baking dish. Cover with half the onions and season well.

4 Place the fish fillets on top of the vegetables and tuck the herbs in between them. Top with the tomato slices and then the remaining onions and potatoes.

5 Pour over the orange juice, white wine and saffron liquid, season with salt and black pepper and drizzle a little extra olive oil on top. Bake the fish uncovered for about 30 minutes, until the potatoes are tender and the fish is cooked.

FRESH TUNA AND TOMATO STEW

This is a deliciously simple Italian fish stew that relies on good basic ingredients. For a complete Italian meal, serve it with polenta or pasta.

INGREDIENTS
12 baby onions, peeled
900g/2lb ripe tomatoes
675g/1½ lb fresh tuna
45ml/3 tbsp olive oil
2 garlic cloves, crushed
45ml/3 tbsp chopped fresh herbs
2 bay leaves
2.5ml/½ tsp caster sugar
30ml/2 tbsp sun-dried tomato purée
150ml/¼ pint/⅔ cup dry white wine
salt and freshly ground black pepper
baby courgettes and fresh herbs,
to garnish

SERVES 4

1 Leave the onions whole and cook them in a pan of boiling water for 4–5 minutes until softened. Drain.

2 Plunge the tomatoes into boiling water for 30 seconds, then refresh them in cold water. Peel away the skins and chop roughly.

3 Cut the tuna into 2.5cm/1in chunks. Heat the olive oil in a large frying or sauté pan and quickly fry the tuna until browned. Drain.

4 Add the onions, tomatoes, garlic, chopped herbs, bay leaves, sugar, sun-dried tomato purée and wine and bring the mixture to the boil, breaking up the tomatoes with a wooden spoon as it cooks.

5 Reduce the heat and simmer the stew gently for about 5 minutes. Add the cooked tuna chunks to the saucepan and cook for a further 5 minutes. Add salt and black pepper to taste, then serve the stew hot, garnished with baby courgettes and fresh herbs.

MOULES MARINIÈRE

This is the best and easiest way to serve the small tender mussels, or *bouchots*, that are farmed along much of the French coastline. Serve with plenty of crusty bread to dip in the juices.

INGREDIENTS
1.75kg/4½lb mussels
300ml/½ pint/1¼ cups dry white wine
4–5 large shallots, finely chopped
bouquet garni
freshly ground black pepper

SERVES 4

1 Discard any broken mussels and those with open shells that refuse to close when tapped. Under cold running water, scrape the mussel shells with a knife to remove any barnacles and pull out the stringy "beards". Soak the mussels in several changes of cold water for at least 1 hour.

2 In a large heavy-based flameproof casserole, combine the wine, shallots, bouquet garni and plenty of black pepper. Bring to a boil over a medium-high heat and cook for 2 minutes.

3 Add the mussels and cook, tightly covered, for about 5 minutes, or until the mussels open, shaking and tossing the pan occasionally. Discard any mussels that do not open.

4 Using a slotted spoon, divide the cooked mussels among individual warmed soup plates. Tilt the casserole a little and hold it for a few seconds to allow any sand to settle to the bottom.

5 Spoon or pour the cooking liquid over the mussels, dividing it evenly, then serve at once.

GRILLED GARLIC MUSSELS

The crunchy crumb topping provides a good contrast to the succulent mussels underneath in this flavoursome French gratin-style dish.

INGREDIENTS
1.5kg/3–3½lb live mussels
120ml/4fl oz/½ cup dry white wine
50g/2oz/4 tbsp butter
2 shallots, finely chopped
2 garlic cloves, crushed
50g/2oz/6 tbsp dried white breadcrumbs
60ml/4 tbsp chopped fresh mixed herbs, such as flat leaf parsley, basil and oregano
30ml/2 tbsp freshly grated Parmesan cheese
salt and ground black pepper
basil leaves, to garnish

SERVES 4

1 Scrub the mussels under cold running water. Remove the beards and discard any mussels that are open. Place in a pan with the wine. Cover and cook over a high heat, shaking the pan occasionally, for 5–8 minutes until the mussels have opened.

2 Strain the mussels and reserve the cooking liquid. Discard any that remain closed. Allow to cool slightly, then remove and discard the top half of each shell, leaving the mussels on the remaining halves.

3 Melt the butter in a large frying pan and fry the shallots until softened. Add the garlic and cook for 1–2 minutes.

4 Stir in the breadcrumbs and cook, stirring, until lightly browned. Remove from the heat and stir in the herbs. Moisten with a little of the reserved mussel liquid, then season to taste with salt and pepper. Preheat the grill.

5 Spoon the breadcrumb mixture over the mussels in their shells and arrange on baking sheets. Sprinkle with the grated Parmesan.

6 Cook the mussels under the hot grill in batches for about 2 minutes, until the topping is crisp and golden. Keep the cooked mussels warm in a low oven while grilling the remainder. Garnish with basil leaves and serve immediately.

CHILLI PRAWNS

This spicy French dish of large prawns with tomatoes and a chopped red chilli makes a lovely light main course for a casual supper. Serve with rice, noodles or freshly cooked pasta and a leafy salad.

INGREDIENTS
45ml/3 tbsp olive oil
2 shallots, chopped
2 garlic cloves, chopped
1 fresh red chilli, chopped
450g/1lb ripe tomatoes, peeled, seeded and chopped
15ml/1 tbsp tomato purée
1 bay leaf
1 thyme sprig
90ml/6 tbsp dry white wine
450g/1lb cooked, peeled large prawns
salt and ground black pepper
roughly torn basil leaves, to garnish

SERVES 3–4

COOK'S TIP
For a milder flavour, remove all the seeds from the chilli.

1 Heat the oil in a pan, then add the shallots, garlic and chilli and fry until the garlic starts to brown.

2 Add the tomatoes, tomato purée, bay leaf, thyme, wine and seasoning. Bring to the boil, then reduce the heat and cook gently for about 10 minutes, stirring occasionally, until the sauce has thickened. Discard the herbs.

3 Stir the prawns into the sauce and heat through for a few minutes. Taste and adjust the seasoning. Scatter over the basil leaves and serve at once.

FISH STEW

R ouille is a classic Provençal sauce traditionally served with fish stews. The broth can be served as a starter and the fish as a main course.

INGREDIENTS
225g/8oz/2 cups cooked unshelled prawns
450g/1lb mixed white fish fillets
45ml/3 tbsp olive oil
1 onion, chopped
1 leek, sliced
1 carrot, diced
1 garlic clove, chopped
2.5ml/½ tsp ground turmeric
150ml/¼ pint/⅔ cup dry white wine
400g/14oz can chopped tomatoes
fresh parsley, thyme and fennel sprigs
small piece of orange peel
1 cleaned squid, sliced
12 live mussels
salt and ground black pepper
*Parmesan cheese shavings and chopped
fresh parsley, to garnish*

FOR THE ROUILLE SAUCE
2 slices white bread, crusts removed
2 garlic cloves, crushed
½ fresh red chilli
15ml/1 tbsp tomato purée
45–60ml/3–4 tbsp olive oil

SERVES 4

1 Peel the prawns leaving the tails on; cover and chill. Place all the prawn and fish trimmings in a pan and cover with 450ml/¾ pint/1⅞ cups water. Bring to the boil, then cover the pan and simmer for 30 minutes. Strain and reserve the stock.

2 Heat the oil in a large saucepan and add the onion, leek, carrot and garlic. Fry gently for 6–7 minutes, stir in the turmeric, wine, tomatoes and juice, fish stock, herbs and orange peel. Bring to the boil, cover, and simmer for about 20 minutes.

3 Meanwhile to make the rouille sauce, process the bread in a food processor or blender with the garlic, chilli and tomato purée. With the motor running, pour in the oil in a thin drizzle until the mixture is smooth and thickened.

4 Add the fish and seafood to the pan and simmer for 5–6 minutes, or until the fish is opaque and the mussels open. Remove the orange peel. Season. Serve in bowls with a spoonful of the rouille sauce and sprinkled with Parmesan and parsley.

MEDITERRANEAN PLAICE ROLLS

Sun-dried tomatoes, pine nuts and anchovies make a flavoursome combination for stuffing these plaice fillets to produce a typical southern French dish.

INGREDIENTS

4 plaice fillets, about 225g/8oz
each, skinned
75g/3oz/6 tbsp butter
1 small onion, chopped
1 celery stick, finely chopped
115g/4oz/2 cups fresh white breadcrumbs
45ml/3 tbsp chopped fresh parsley
30ml/2 tbsp pine nuts, toasted
3–4 pieces sun-dried tomatoes in oil,
drained and chopped
50g/2oz can anchovy fillets, drained
and chopped
75ml/5 tbsp fish stock
ground black pepper

SERVES 4

1 Preheat the oven to 180°C/350°F/Gas 4. Cut the plaice fillets in half lengthways to make eight smaller fillets.

2 Melt the butter in a pan and add the onion and celery. Cover and cook for 15 minutes, until soft. Do not brown.

3 Combine the breadcrumbs, parsley, pine nuts, sun-dried tomatoes and anchovies. Stir in the softened vegetables with the buttery juices and season with pepper.

4 Divide the stuffing into eight portions. Taking one portion at a time, form the stuffing into balls, then roll up each one inside a plaice fillet. Secure each roll with a cocktail stick.

5 Place the rolled-up fillets in a buttered ovenproof dish. Pour in the stock and cover the dish with a piece of buttered foil. Bake for about 20 minutes, or until the fish flakes easily when tested with a fork. Remove the cocktail sticks, then serve the plaice rolls with a little of the cooking juices drizzled over.

MUSSELS WITH SPAGHETTI

M ussels are popular in all the coastal regions of Italy, and are delicious with pasta. If you like, reserve a few in their half-shells for decoration.

INGREDIENTS
1kg/2¼lb fresh mussels, in their shells
400g/14oz spaghetti
75ml/5 tbsp olive oil
3 garlic cloves, finely chopped
60ml/4 tbsp chopped fresh parsley
60ml/4 tbsp white wine
salt and ground black pepper

SERVES 4

1 Scrub the mussels well under cold running water, pulling off the "beard" with a small sharp knife.

2 Bring a large pan of water to the boil for the pasta. Place the mussels with a cupful of water in another large saucepan over a moderate heat. As soon as they open, lift them out one by one.

3 When all the mussels have opened (discard any that do not), strain the liquid in the saucepan through a layer of kitchen paper into a bowl and set aside until needed. Add salt to the pan of boiling water, and add the spaghetti.

4 Meanwhile, heat the oil in large frying pan. Add the garlic and parsley, and cook for 2–3 minutes. Add the mussels, the reserved juice and the wine and simmer very gently. Add a generous amount of freshly ground black pepper, then taste for seasoning and add salt, if necessary.

5 Drain the spaghetti when it is *al dente*. Tip it into the frying pan with the sauce, and stir well over a moderate heat for a few minutes more, then serve at once.

Red Mullet with Fennel

Whole mullet are excellent cooked in this way – you'll need only two fish if they are large. Fennel is a classic French accompaniment to red mullet; the lemon butter sets off both flavours.

Ingredients
3 small fennel bulbs
60ml/4 tbsp olive oil
2 small onions, thinly sliced
2–4 basil leaves
4 small or 2 large red mullet, cleaned
grated rind of ½ lemon
150ml/¼ pint/⅔ cup fish stock
50g/2oz/4 tbsp butter
juice of 1 lemon

Serves 4

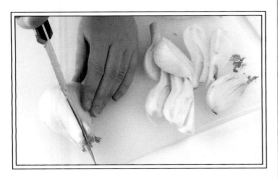

1 Snip off the feathery fronds from the fennel chop finely and reserve for the garnish. Cut the fennel into wedges, leaving the layers attached at the root ends.

2 Heat the oil in a frying pan large enough to take the fish in a single layer. Add the fennel and onions and cook for 10–15 minutes, until softened and lightly browned.

3 Tuck a basil leaf inside each red mullet, then place the fish on top of the vegetables in the frying pan. Sprinkle the lemon rind over the fish. Pour in the stock and bring just to the boil. Cover the pan and cook gently for 15–20 minutes, until the fish are just tender.

4 Melt the butter in a small pan and, when it starts to sizzle and colour slightly, add the lemon juice. Pour the sauce over the fish, sprinkle with the reserved fennel fronds and serve immediately.

BOUILLABAISSE

Different variations of this French fish stew are found along the Mediterranean coast. Almost any fish and shellfish can be used.

INGREDIENTS
2.7kg/6lb white fish, such as sea bass,
snapper or monkfish, filleted and skinned
45ml/3 tbsp extra virgin olive oil
grated rind of 1 orange
1 garlic clove, very finely chopped
pinch of saffron threads
30ml/2 tbsp pastis
1 small fennel bulb, finely chopped
1 large onion, finely chopped
2.4 litres/4 pints/10 cups well-flavoured
fish stock
225g/8oz small new potatoes, sliced
900g/2lb large raw Mediterranean
prawns, peeled
croûtons, to serve

FOR THE ROUILLE
25g/1oz/⅔ cup soft white breadcrumbs
1–2 garlic cloves, very finely chopped
½ red pepper, roasted
5ml/1 tsp tomato purée
120ml/4fl oz/½ cup extra virgin olive oil

SERVES 8

1 Using a sharp knife, cut the white fish fillets into serving pieces, and place them in a mixing bowl with 30ml/2 tbsp of the olive oil, the orange rind, chopped garlic, saffron threads and pastis. Turn the mixture to coat well, then cover and chill.

2 To make the rouille, first soak the breadcrumbs in a bowl of cold water, then squeeze them till they are dry. Place the breadcrumbs in a food processor or blender with the chopped garlic, roasted red pepper and tomato purée and process until it forms a smooth mixture.

3 With the food processor or blender machine running, slowly pour the olive oil through the feed tube, scraping down the sides once or twice. Set aside while you cook the fish.

4 To finish the bouillabaisse, heat the remaining 15ml/1 tbsp of olive oil in a wide flameproof casserole over a medium heat. Cook the fennel bulb and onion for about 5 minutes until the onion just softens, then add the stock.

5 Bring to the boil, add the potatoes and cook for about 5–7 minutes. Reduce the heat back to medium and begin to add the fish, starting with the thickest pieces and adding the thinner ones after 2–3 minutes. Add the prawns and continue to simmer very gently until all the fish and shellfish are fully cooked.

6 Transfer the fish, shellfish and potatoes to a heated tureen or individual soup plates. Adjust the seasoning to taste and ladle the soup over. Serve with croûtons spread with the rouille.

CHUNKY SEAFOOD STEW

This is a versatile Spanish stew in which many different combinations of fish and shellfish may be used. Only ever buy absolutely fresh fish.

INGREDIENTS

45ml/3 tbsp olive oil
2 large onions, chopped
1 small green pepper, seeded and sliced
3 carrots, chopped
3 garlic cloves, crushed
30ml/2 tbsp tomato purée
2 x 400g/14oz cans chopped tomatoes
45ml/3 tbsp chopped fresh parsley
5ml/1 tsp fresh thyme, or 1.5ml/¼ tsp dried thyme
15ml/1 tbsp chopped fresh basil, or 5ml/1 tsp dried basil
120ml/4fl oz/½ cup dry white wine
450g/1lb raw prawns, peeled and deveined, or cooked peeled prawns
1.5kg/3–3½lb live mussels or clams, or a mixture of both, thoroughly cleaned
900g/2lb halibut or other firm, white fish fillets, cut into 5–7.5cm/2–3in pieces
350ml/12fl oz/1½ cups fish stock or water
salt and ground black pepper
chopped fresh herbs, to garnish

SERVES 6

1 Heat the oil in a flameproof casserole. Add the onions, green pepper, carrots and garlic and cook until the vegetables are tender, about 5 minutes.

2 Add the tomato purée, canned tomatoes, herbs and wine and stir well to combine. Bring to the boil and simmer for 20 minutes.

3 Add the raw prawns, if using, mussels or clams, fish pieces and stock or water. Season with salt and pepper.

4 Bring back to the boil, then simmer for about 5–6 minutes, until the prawns turn pink, the fish flakes easily and the mussels and clams open. If using cooked prawns, add these for the last 2 minutes.

5 Ladle into large, warmed soup plates and serve garnished with a sprinkling of chopped fresh herbs.

> ### COOK'S TIP
> Before cooking, discard any shellfish that remain open when tapped. After cooking, discard any that remain closed.

Poultry and Meat

Chicken is extremely popular throughout Europe, either cooked whole or in pieces, or in the form of poussins. Other poultry such as pheasant, quail and duck is also eaten, as are pork, rabbit and lamb, which feature prominently in the cuisine of the south and west Mediterranean countries, although beef is less frequently found on the menu.

Chicken is cooked in an enormous variety of ways, often flavoured with typical Mediterranean ingredients, such as olives, grapes, fennel, juniper, peppers and tomatoes.

Lamb features strongly in the cooking of Greece, even in the form of sausages, and is well-known as an ingredient of moussaka and kleftiko.

CHICKEN IN PIZZAIOLA SAUCE

The popular Italian combination of sweet red pepper and sun-dried tomatoes creates a wonderful, colourful sauce for the chicken.

INGREDIENTS
30ml/2 tbsp plain flour
4 chicken portions (legs, breasts or quarters)
30ml/2 tbsp olive oil
1 onion, chopped
2 garlic cloves, chopped
1 red pepper, seeded and chopped
400g/14oz can chopped tomatoes
30ml/2 tbsp red pesto sauce
4 sun-dried tomatoes in oil, chopped
150ml/¼ pint/⅔ cup chicken stock
5ml/1 tsp dried oregano
8 black olives, stoned
salt and ground black pepper
fresh basil sprigs, to garnish
tagliatelle, to serve

SERVES 4

1 Put the flour in a polythene bag and season. Add the chicken and coat well. Heat the oil in a flameproof casserole, and brown the chicken, then remove.

2 Lower the heat, add the onion, garlic and pepper and cook for 5 minutes. Stir in all the remaining ingredients except the olives and bring to the boil.

3 Return the browned chicken portions to the casserole, season lightly, cover and simmer for 30–35 minutes, or until the chicken is cooked.

4 Add the olives and simmer for a further 5 minutes. Transfer to a warmed serving dish, and garnish with the fresh basil sprigs. Serve hot with tagliatelle.

CHICKEN WITH OLIVES

This tasty Italian dish makes a good light main course and can be put together quickly for unexpected guests. It is equally good with turkey pieces.

INGREDIENTS
90ml/6 tbsp olive oil
1 garlic clove, crushed
1 dried chilli, lightly crushed
500g/1¼lb boneless chicken breast, cut into 5mm/¼in slices
120ml/4fl oz/½ cup dry white wine
4 tomatoes, peeled and seeded, cut into thin strips
24 black olives
6–8 fresh basil leaves, torn into pieces, and basil sprigs, to garnish
salt and ground black pepper

SERVES 4

1 Heat 60ml/4 tbsp of the olive oil in a large frying pan. Add the garlic and dried chilli, and cook over a low heat until the garlic is golden.

2 Raise the heat to moderate. Place the chicken in the pan, and brown all over for about 2 minutes. Season.

3 Transfer the chicken to a heated dish. Remove the garlic and chilli and discard. Add the wine, tomato strips and olives, then cook over a moderate heat for 3–4 minutes. Using a wooden spoon, scrape up any meat residue from the base of the pan.

4 Return the chicken to the pan, and sprinkle with the fresh basil leaves. Heat for about 30 seconds, to make sure it is warmed through, then serve, garnished with basil sprigs.

POUSSINS WITH GRAPES IN VERMOUTH

I n France, grapes are often included in savoury dishes. The herbs used to flavour vermouth, combined with the grapes, make a beautiful sauce.

INGREDIENTS
4 oven-ready poussins, about
450g/1lb each
50g/2oz/4 tbsp butter, softened
2 shallots, chopped
60ml/4 tbsp chopped fresh parsley
225g/8oz white grapes, preferably
muscatel, halved and seeded
150ml/¼ pint/⅔ cup dry white vermouth
5ml/1 tsp cornflour
60ml/4 tbsp double cream
salt and ground black pepper
30ml/2 tbsp pine nuts, toasted
watercress sprigs, to garnish

SERVES 4

1 Preheat the oven to 200°C/400°F/Gas 6. Wash and dry the poussins. Spread the softened butter all over the birds and put a hazelnut-size piece in the cavity of each bird. Mix together the shallots and parsley.

2 Place a quarter of the shallot mixture inside each bird. Put them in a roasting tin and roast for 40–50 minutes, or until the juices run clear when the thickest part of the flesh is pierced with a skewer. Transfer to a warmed platter and keep warm.

3 Skim off most of the fat from the tin, then add the grapes and vermouth. Place the tin over a low heat for a few minutes to warm the grapes.

4 Lift the grapes out of the tin with a slotted spoon and scatter them around the birds. Keep covered. Stir the cornflour into the cream, then add to the pan juices. Cook gently for a few minutes, stirring, until the sauce has thickened. Taste and adjust the seasoning.

5 Pour the sauce around the poussins. Sprinkle with the toasted pine nuts and garnish with watercress sprigs.

PHEASANT WITH APPLE SAUCE

N ormandy is famed for its dairy farms and apple orchards. This recipe, with its apples, cider, Calvados, butter and cream, makes the most of its produce.

INGREDIENTS
2 oven-ready pheasants
15ml/1 tbsp olive oil
25g/1oz/2 tbsp butter
60ml/4 tbsp Calvados
450ml/¾ pint/1⅞ cups dry cider
bouquet garni
3 eating apples, peeled, cored and
thickly sliced
150ml/¼ pint/⅔ cup double cream
salt and ground black pepper
thyme sprigs, to garnish

SERVES 4

1 Preheat the oven to 160°C/325°F/Gas 3. Joint both pheasants into four pieces. Discard the backbones and knuckles.

2 Heat the oil and butter in a large flameproof casserole. Working in two batches, add the pheasant pieces to the casserole and brown them over a high heat. Once browned return all the pheasant pieces to the casserole.

3 Standing well back, pour the Calvados over the pheasant pieces and set it alight. When the flames have subsided, pour in the cider, then add the bouquet garni and seasoning and bring to the boil. Cover and cook for 50 minutes.

4 Tuck the apple slices around the pheasant. Cover and cook for 5–10 minutes, or until the pheasant is tender. Transfer the pheasant and apple slices to a warmed serving plate, cover and keep warm. Remove the bouquet garni.

5 Reduce the sauce by half, stir in the cream and simmer for 2–3 minutes until thickened. Spoon over the pheasant and serve at once, garnished with thyme sprigs.

ROAST CHICKEN WITH FENNEL

In Tuscany this dish is prepared with wild fennel. Cultivated fennel bulbs work just as well.

INGREDIENTS

1.5kg/3–3½ lb roasting chicken
1 onion, quartered
120ml/4fl oz/½ cup extra virgin olive oil
2 fennel bulbs
1 garlic clove, peeled
pinch of grated nutmeg
3–4 thin slices of pancetta or
rindless smoked streaky bacon
120ml/4fl oz/½ cup dry white wine
salt and ground black pepper

SERVES 4–5

1 Preheat the oven to 180°C/350°F/Gas 4. Rinse the chicken in cold water. Pat it dry inside and out with kitchen paper. Sprinkle the cavity with salt and pepper, then place the onion quarters inside. Rub the chicken flesh with about 45ml/3 tbsp of the olive oil. Place in a roasting tin.

2 Cut the feathery green fronds from the tops of the fennel bulbs. Chop the fronds with the garlic. Place in a small bowl and mix with the grated nutmeg. Season with salt and pepper.

3 Sprinkle the fennel mixture over the chicken, pressing it on to the oiled skin. Cover the breast with the slices of pancetta or bacon. Sprinkle with 30ml/2 tbsp of the remaining olive oil. Roast for 30 minutes.

4 Meanwhile, boil or steam the fennel bulbs until barely tender. Remove from the heat and cut lengthways into quarters or sixths. Remove the chicken from the oven and baste it, then arrange the fennel pieces around it. Drizzle the fennel with the remaining oil.

5 Pour about half the wine over the chicken, and return the pan to the oven. Roast the chicken for 30 minutes more, then baste it again. Pour on the remaining wine. Cook for 15–20 minutes more, or until the chicken is cooked through. To test, prick the thigh with a fork. If the juices run clear, the chicken is ready. Transfer it to a serving platter, and arrange the fennel around it. Serve immediately.

PAN-FRIED MARINATED POUSSINS

oultry is very important in the cooking of Tuscany and these small birds are bursting with flavour.

INGREDIENTS

2 poussins, about 450g/1lb each
5–6 mint leaves, torn into pieces
1 leek, sliced into thin rings
1 garlic clove, finely chopped
60ml/4 tbsp extra virgin olive oil
30ml/2 tbsp freshly squeezed lemon juice
50ml/2fl oz/¼ cup dry white wine
salt and ground black pepper
mint leaves, to garnish

SERVES 3–4

1 Cut both poussins in half down the backbone, dividing the breast. Flatten the four halves with a mallet. Place them in a bowl with the mint, leek rings and garlic. Add a generous sprinkling of pepper. Sprinkle with the oil and half the lemon juice, cover, and allow to stand in a cool place for 6 hours.

2 Heat a large heavy-based frying pan. Place the poussins and marinade in the pan, cover, and cook over a medium heat for about 45 minutes. Season with salt. Transfer the poussins to a heated serving platter.

3 Tilt the pan and spoon off any surface fat. Pour in the wine and remaining lemon juice, and cook until the sauce reduces by about half *(right)*. Strain the sauce, pressing the vegetables to extract all the juices. Place the poussin halves on individual heated plates, and spoon over the sauce. Garnish with the mint leaves and serve at once.

TUSCAN CHICKEN

This simple peasant casserole has all the flavours of traditional Tuscan ingredients. The wine can be replaced by chicken stock, if preferred.

INGREDIENTS
15ml/1 tbsp extra virgin olive oil
8 chicken thighs, skinned
1 onion, thinly sliced
2 red peppers, seeded and sliced
1 garlic clove, crushed
300ml/½ pint/1¼ cups passata (puréed tomatoes)
150ml/¼ pint/⅔ cup dry white wine
1 large oregano sprig, or
5ml/1 tsp dried oregano
400g/14oz can cannellini beans, drained
45ml/3 tbsp fresh white breadcrumbs
salt and ground black pepper
fresh oregano, to garnish

SERVES 4

COOK'S TIP
When herbs are abundant, stir in a handful of fresh oregano leaves just before sprinkling with the breadcrumbs.

1 Heat the oil in a heavy-based frying pan which can be used under the grill.

2 Cook the chicken until golden. Remove and keep hot. Add the onion and peppers to the pan and sauté gently until softened. Stir in the garlic. Return the chicken to the pan. Add the tomatoes, wine and oregano, and salt and pepper.

3 Bring to the boil. Cover the pan tightly, lower the heat and simmer for 30–35 minutes or until the chicken is tender.

4 When the chicken is thoroughly cooked, stir in the cannellini beans. Cover the pan again and raise the heat slightly. Leave to simmer for about 5 minutes more, stirring once or twice, until the beans are hot. Preheat the grill.

5 Sprinkle the breadcrumbs evenly over the mixture in the pan and grill until the crumb topping is golden brown. Serve immediately, garnished with fresh oregano.

QUAIL WITH GRAPES

Fresh quail are a favourite food in Florence and other Tuscan cities. Use flavourful seedless green grapes for this recipe.

INGREDIENTS
6–8 oven-ready fresh quail
60ml/4 tbsp olive oil
50g/2oz/¼ cup diced pancetta or rindless smoked streaky bacon
250ml/8fl oz/1 cup dry white wine
250ml/8fl oz/1 cup hot chicken stock
350g/12oz bunch of green grapes
salt and ground black pepper

SERVES 4

1 Wash the quail carefully inside and out with cold water. Pat dry with kitchen paper, then sprinkle salt and pepper into the cavities.

2 Heat the oil in a heavy-based frying pan or casserole large enough to hold all the quail in a single layer. Stir in the pancetta or bacon, and cook over a low heat for 5 minutes.

3 Raise the heat to moderate, and place the quail in the pan. Brown them evenly on all sides. Pour in the wine, and cook over a medium heat until the liquid reduces by about half. Turn the quail over. Cover the pan, and cook for 10–15 minutes more. Add the stock, turn the quail again, cover, and cook for 15–20 minutes, or until the birds are tender. Remove to a warmed serving platter with tongs and keep hot while the sauce is being finished.

4 Bring a saucepan of water to the boil. Drop in the bunch of grapes, and blanch for about 3 minutes. Drain, then pull the grapes from the stem and set aside.

5 Strain the pan juices into a small glass jug. Spoon off any fat from the surface. Pour the strained gravy into a small saucepan. Add the grapes and warm them gently for 2–3 minutes. Spoon around the quail and serve.

ROAST PHEASANT WITH JUNIPER BERRIES

Sage and juniper are often used in Tuscan cooking to flavour pheasant and other game birds.

INGREDIENTS

1.2–1.4kg/2½–3lb oven-ready pheasant

45ml/3 tbsp olive oil

2 sage sprigs

3 shallots, chopped

1 bay leaf

2 lemon quarters, plus

5ml/1 tsp lemon juice

30ml/2 tbsp juniper berries, crushed

4 thin slices pancetta or streaky bacon

90ml/6 tbsp dry white wine

250ml/8fl oz/1 cup hot chicken stock

25g/1oz/2 tbsp butter, at
room temperature

30ml/2 tbsp plain flour

30ml/2 tbsp brandy

salt and ground black pepper

SERVES 3–4

1 Rub the pheasant with 15ml/1 tbsp of the olive oil. Place the remaining oil, sage leaves, shallots and bay leaf in a shallow bowl. Stir in the lemon juice and juniper berries. Add the pheasant and lemon quarters to the bowl and spoon the marinade over.

2 Cover the dish and allow to stand for several hours in a cool place, turning the pheasant occasionally.

3 Preheat the oven to 180°C/350°F/Gas 4. Place the pheasant in a roasting tin, reserving the marinade. Sprinkle the cavity with salt and pepper. Remove the lemon quarters and bay leaf from the marinade and tuck them inside the bird. Arrange some of the sage leaves from the marinade on the pheasant breast, and lay the pancetta or bacon over the top. Secure with string. Spoon the rest of the marinade and the wine over the pheasant.

4 Roast for about 30 minutes per 450g/1lb, until tender. Baste frequently with the pan juices. Transfer to a serving platter and discard the string and pancetta or bacon.

5 Tilt the roasting tin and skim off any surface fat. Add the stock. Stir over a medium heat, scraping up any residues, then bring to the boil and cook for a few minutes. Strain into a saucepan. Mix the butter to a paste with the flour. Stir into the gravy, a little at a time, then boil for 2–3 minutes, stirring constantly. Remove from the heat, stir in the brandy, and serve in a gravy boat with the pheasant.

DUCK WITH CHESTNUT SAUCE

his autumnal dish makes use of the sweet chestnuts that are gathered in Italian woods.

INGREDIENTS
1 rosemary sprig
1 garlic clove, thinly sliced
30ml/2 tbsp extra virgin olive oil
4 duck breasts, boned and trimmed
rosemary sprigs, to garnish

FOR THE SAUCE
450g/1lb chestnuts
5ml/1 tsp extra virgin olive oil
350ml/12fl oz/1½ cups milk
1 small onion, finely chopped
1 carrot, finely chopped
1 small bay leaf
30ml/2 tbsp single cream

SERVES 4–5

1 Strip the leaves from the rosemary sprig. Mix them with the garlic and oil in a shallow bowl. Pat the duck breasts dry with kitchen paper. Brush the duck breasts with the marinade and allow to stand for at least 2 hours before cooking.

2 Preheat the oven to 180°C/350°F/Gas 4. Make the sauce. Cut a cross in the flat side of each chestnut with a sharp knife. Place them in a roasting tin with the oil, shaking the pan to coat the nuts thoroughly. Bake for about 20 minutes, then peel.

3 Tip the peeled chestnuts into a heavy-based saucepan and add the milk, onion, carrot and bay leaf. Cook over a low heat for 10–15 minutes until the chestnuts are very tender.

4 Preheat the grill, or prepare a barbecue. Press the chestnut mixture through a sieve into a clean pan. Stir in the cream. Place over a low heat, stirring occasionally.

5 Grill the duck breasts for 6–8 minutes, turning once, until medium rare. The meat should be pink when sliced.

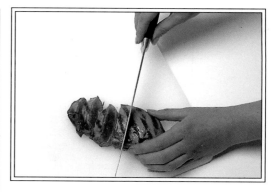

6 Slice the duck into rounds and fan out on heated plates. Garnish with rosemary sprigs and add a portion of chestnut sauce to each plate.

COOK'S TIP
The chestnut sauce can be prepared in advance and kept in the fridge for up to two days, or made when chestnuts are in season and frozen without the cream. Thaw to room temperature before reheating, adding enough single cream to give the consistency of puréed potatoes.

CHICKEN WITH CHORIZO

The addition of chorizo sausage and sherry gives a warm and interesting flavour to this Spanish dish.

INGREDIENTS
1.5kg/3–3½lb chicken, jointed, or
4 chicken legs, halved and skinned
10ml/2 tsp paprika
60ml/4 tbsp olive oil
2 small onions, sliced
6 garlic cloves, thinly sliced
150g/5oz chorizo sausage, thickly sliced
400g/14oz can chopped tomatoes
2 bay leaves
75ml/3fl oz/⅓ cup medium sherry
salt and ground black pepper
boiled potatoes, to serve

SERVES 4

1 Preheat the oven to 190°C/375°F/Gas 5. Coat the chicken pieces in the paprika and season lightly with salt.

2 Heat the olive oil in a frying pan and fry the chicken on all sides to brown. With a slotted spoon, transfer the chicken pieces to an ovenproof dish.

3 Add the onions to the pan and fry quickly until golden. Add the garlic and chorizo and fry for 2 minutes. (Don't burn the garlic, or it will taste bitter.)

VARIATION
Use pork chump chops or leg steaks instead of the chicken and reduce the cooking time slightly.

4 Add the tomatoes, bay leaves and sherry and bring to the boil. Pour over the chicken and cover with a lid. Bake in the oven for 45 minutes. Remove the lid and season to taste with salt and pepper. Cook for a further 20 minutes until the chicken is tender and golden. Serve with potatoes.

CHICKEN CASSEROLE WITH SPICED FIGS

he Catalans have various recipes for fruit with meat, and this is an unusual dish that uses fresh figs.

INGREDIENTS
FOR THE FIGS
150g/5oz/¾ cup granulated sugar
120ml/4fl oz/½ cup white wine vinegar
1 slice lemon
1 cinnamon stick
450g/1lb fresh figs

FOR THE CHICKEN
120ml/4fl oz/½ cup medium sweet
white wine
rind of ½ lemon
1.5kg/3–3½lb chicken, jointed into
eight pieces
50g/2oz lardons or thick streaky bacon,
cut into strips
15ml/1 tbsp olive oil
50ml/2fl oz/¼ cup chicken stock
salt and ground black pepper
green salad, to serve (optional)

SERVES 4

1 Bring 120ml/4fl oz/½ cup water to the boil with the sugar, vinegar, lemon and cinnamon. Simmer for 5 minutes. Add the figs; simmer for 10 minutes. Remove from the heat, cover, and set aside overnight.

2 Preheat the oven to 180°C/350°F/Gas 4. Drain the figs and place in a bowl. Add the wine and lemon rind to the figs. Season the chicken. In a large, shallow ovenproof dish, cook the lardons or bacon until the fat runs and they turn golden. Remove, leaving the oil in the pan. Add the olive oil and brown the chicken pieces.

3 Strain the figs and add the wine to the chicken. Boil until reduced and syrupy. Transfer the dish to the oven and cook, uncovered, for 20 minutes. Add the figs with the chicken stock, cover the dish, and return to the oven for a further 10 minutes. Serve the chicken and figs with a green salad, if liked.

POT-ROAST POUSSINS

This method of cooking keeps the poussins moist and succulent, and provides a whole meal cooked in one dish. The fresh herbs used are typical of southern France.

INGREDIENTS
15ml/1 tbsp olive oil
1 onion, sliced
1 large garlic clove, sliced
50g/2oz/½ cup diced lightly
smoked bacon
2 fresh poussins, just under 450g/1lb each
30ml/2 tbsp butter, melted
2 baby celery hearts, each cut into 4
8 baby carrots
2 small courgettes, cut into chunks
8 small new potatoes
600ml/1 pint/2½ cups chicken stock
150ml/¼ pint/⅔ cup dry white wine
1 bay leaf
2 fresh thyme sprigs
2 fresh rosemary sprigs
15ml/1 tbsp butter, softened
15ml/1 tbsp plain flour
salt and ground black pepper
fresh herbs, to garnish

SERVES 2-4

1 Preheat the oven to 190°C/375°F/Gas 5. Heat the olive oil in a large flameproof casserole, add the onion, garlic and bacon and sauté for 5–6 minutes.

2 Brush the poussins with a little of the melted butter and season well. Lay them on top of the onion mixture and arrange the prepared vegetables around them. Pour the chicken stock and wine around the birds and add the herbs. Cover, bake for 20 minutes, then remove the lid and brush the birds with the remaining melted butter. Bake for a further 25–30 minutes until golden.

3 Transfer the poussins to warmed serving plates. Remove the vegetables with a slotted spoon and arrange them round the birds. Cover with foil and keep warm.

4 Discard the herbs from the pan juices. In a bowl, mix together the butter and flour to form a thick paste. Bring the liquid in the pan to the boil and then whisk in a few teaspoonfuls of the paste, until thickened. Taste the sauce for seasoning and add salt and pepper if necessary. Serve the poussins, cut in half if wished, with the vegetables. Garnish with fresh herb sprigs.

CHICKEN WITH LEMON AND GARLIC

asy to cook and delicious to eat, this Spanish dish is served with fried potatoes and aioli.

INGREDIENTS
225g/8oz skinless chicken breast fillets
30ml/2 tbsp olive oil
1 shallot, finely chopped
4 garlic cloves, finely chopped
5ml/1 tsp paprika
juice of 1 lemon
30ml/2 tbsp chopped fresh parsley
salt and freshly ground black pepper
flat leaf parsley, to garnish
lemon wedges, to serve

SERVES 4

COOK'S TIP
For a variation on this dish, try using strips of turkey breast or pork.

1 Sandwich the chicken breasts between two sheets of greaseproof paper or clear film. Pound with the flat side of a meat hammer or roll out with a rolling pin until the fillets are about 5mm/¼in thick.

2 Cut the chicken into strips about 1cm/½in wide. Heat the oil in a large frying pan. Stir-fry the chicken strips with the shallot, garlic and paprika over a high heat for about 6–8 minutes, until lightly browned and cooked through. Add the lemon juice and parsley with salt and pepper to taste. Garnish with parsley and serve hot with lemon wedges.

CHICKEN KEBABS

hicken kebabs are a great favourite all over Greece. They are ideal for summer barbecues.

INGREDIENTS
1 large onion, grated
2 garlic cloves, crushed
120ml/4fl oz/½ cup olive oil
juice of 1 lemon
5ml/1 tsp paprika
2–3 saffron strands, soaked in
15ml/1 tbsp boiling water
2 young chickens
salt and freshly ground black pepper
pitta bread, to serve

SERVES 6–8

1 Mix the onion, garlic, olive oil, lemon juice, paprika and saffron, and season with salt and pepper.

2 Cut the chicken into small pieces, removing the bone if preferred, and place in a shallow bowl. Pour the marinade over the chicken, turning the chicken so that all the pieces are covered evenly. Cover the bowl loosely with clear film and leave in a cool place to marinate for at least 2 hours.

VARIATION
You could remove the boneless chicken from the metal skewers and serve it in pitta bread as a sandwich accompanied by a garlicky yogurt sauce.

3 Thread the chicken on to long kebab sticks. The kebabs can be barbecued or cooked under a moderately hot grill for 10–15 minutes, or until the juices run clear when the meat is pierced. Turn them every now and then. Serve with warm pitta bread.

BRAISED CHICKEN WITH OLIVES

O live groves are a familiar part of the Greek landscape. Here, olives are combined with chicken in a Greek dish that is perfect for entertaining.

INGREDIENTS
30ml/2 tbsp olive oil
1 chicken, about 1.5kg/3–3½ lb
1 large onion, sliced
15ml/1 tbsp grated fresh root ginger
3 garlic cloves, crushed
5ml/1 tsp paprika
250ml/8fl oz/1 cup chicken stock
2–3 saffron strands, soaked in
15ml/1 tbsp boiling water
4–5 spring onions, chopped
15–20 black and green olives, stoned
juice of ½ lemon
salt and freshly ground black pepper
rice and mixed salad, to serve (optional)

SERVES 4

1 Heat the oil in a large saucepan or flameproof casserole and sauté the chicken on all sides until golden.

2 Add the onion, fresh ginger, garlic, paprika and seasoning, and continue frying over a moderate heat, coating the chicken with the mixture.

3 Add the chicken stock and saffron and bring to the boil. Cover and simmer gently for 45 minutes, or until the chicken is well done and the meat comes away from the bone easily.

4 Add the spring onions and cook for a further 15 minutes until the sauce is reduced to about 120ml/4fl oz/½ cup.

5 Add the black and green olives and the lemon juice to the saucepan, stir and continue to cook gently for approximately 5 minutes more.

6 Remove the chicken and place it on a large deep serving plate. Carefully pour over the sauce. Serve with rice and a mixed salad, if liked.

SPICED DUCK WITH PEARS

This delicious casserole is based on a Catalan dish that uses goose or duck. The sautéed pears are added towards the end of cooking along with *picarda* sauce, a pounded pine nut and garlic paste which both flavours and thickens the dish.

INGREDIENTS
6 duck portions, either breast or leg
15ml/1 tbsp olive oil
1 large onion, thinly sliced
1 cinnamon stick, halved
2 thyme sprigs
450ml/¾ pint/1⅞ cups chicken stock

TO FINISH
3 firm, ripe pears
30ml/2 tbsp olive oil
2 garlic cloves, sliced
25g/1oz/¼ cup pine nuts
2.5ml/½ tsp saffron strands
25g/1oz/3 tbsp raisins
salt and ground black pepper
parsley or thyme sprigs, to garnish
mashed potatoes, to serve

SERVES 6

1 Preheat the oven to 180°C/350°F/Gas 4. Fry the duck portions in the oil for about 5 minutes until the skin is golden. Transfer the duck to an ovenproof dish and drain off all but 15ml/1 tbsp of the fat left in the pan.

2 Add the sliced onion to the pan and fry for 5 minutes. Add the cinnamon stick, thyme and stock and bring to the boil. Pour over the duck portions and bake in the oven for 1¼ hours.

COOK'S TIP
A good stock is essential for this dish. Buy a large duck (plus two extra duck breasts if you want generous portions) and joint it yourself, using the giblets and carcass to make stock. Alternatively, buy duck portions and a carton of fresh chicken stock.

3 Meanwhile, halve the pears and fry quickly in the oil until they begin to turn golden on the cut sides. Using a pestle and mortar, pound the garlic, pine nuts and saffron to make a thick, smooth paste.

4 Add the paste to the casserole along with the raisins and pears. Bake in the oven for a further 15 minutes until the pear halves are tender.

5 Season to taste and garnish with parsley or thyme. Serve the duck hot, with mashed potatoes.

CHICKEN WITH HAM AND RICE

This colourful Spanish one-pan dish is ideal for entertaining as it needs no last-minute preparation. Serve with a crisp mixed green salad.

INGREDIENTS

15g/¹⁄₂oz/2 tbsp plain flour
10ml/2 tsp paprika
2.5ml/¹⁄₂ tsp salt
16 chicken drumsticks
60ml/4 tbsp olive oil
1.2 litres/2 pints/5 cups chicken stock
1 onion, finely chopped
2 garlic cloves, crushed
450g/1lb/generous 2¹⁄₄ cups long grain rice
2 bay leaves
225g/8oz/2 cups diced cooked ham
115g/4oz/1 cup pimiento-stuffed green olives
1 green pepper, seeded and diced
2 x 400g/14oz cans chopped tomatoes, with their juice
parsley sprigs, to garnish

SERVES 8

1 Preheat the oven to 180°C/350°F/Gas 4. Shake together the flour, paprika and salt in a plastic bag, add the drumsticks and toss to coat all over.

2 Heat the oil in a large flameproof casserole and, working in batches, brown the chicken slowly on all sides. Remove and keep warm.

3 Meanwhile, bring the stock to the boil and add the onion, crushed garlic, rice and bay leaves. Cook for 10 minutes. Draw aside and add the ham, olives, pepper and canned tomatoes with their juice. Transfer to a shallow ovenproof dish.

4 Arrange the chicken on top, cover and bake for 30–40 minutes or until tender. Add a little more stock if necessary to prevent drying out. Remove the bay leaves and serve garnished with parsley.

BARBECUED LAMB WITH POTATO SLICES

A traditional mixture of fresh herbs adds a summer flavour to this dish. It is designed for the barbecue, a common cooking method in Greece.

INGREDIENTS
1 leg of lamb, about 1.75kg/4–4½ lb
1 garlic clove, sliced
handful each of fresh flat leaf parsley,
sage, rosemary and thyme sprigs
90ml/6 tbsp dry sherry
60ml/4 tbsp walnut oil
500g/1¼lb potatoes
salt and freshly ground black pepper

SERVES 4

1 Place the lamb on a board, smooth side downwards so that you can see where the bone lies. Using a sharp knife, make a long cut through the flesh down to the bone.

2 Scrape away the meat from the bone on both sides, until the bone is completely exposed. Remove the bone and cut away any sinews and excess fat.

3 Cut through the thickest part of the meat to enable it to open out as flat as possible. Make several cuts in the lamb with a sharp knife, and push slivers of garlic and some of the herb sprigs into them.

4 Place the meat in a bowl and pour over the sherry and oil. Chop about half the remaining herbs and scatter over the meat. Cover and leave to marinate in the fridge for at least 30 minutes.

5 Remove the lamb from the marinade and season. Place on a medium-hot barbecue and cook for 30–35 minutes, turning occasionally and basting with the reserved marinade. Alternatively, preheat the oven to 200°C/400°F/Gas 6, and place the lamb in an ovenproof dish in the oven. Cook in the same way.

6 Scrub the potatoes, then cut them into thick slices. Brush them with the marinade and place them around the lamb. Continue cooking for about 15–20 minutes, turning occasionally, until the meat and potatoes are golden brown. Serve at once.

COOK'S TIP
A leg of lamb is easier to cook if it is boned, or "butterflied", first.

MILANESE VEAL

Ossobuco means "hollow bone", and this dish calls for shin of veal cut into sections across the bone. Each bone should have its centre of marrow, which is considered a great delicacy.

INGREDIENTS
50g/2oz/4 tbsp butter
1 garlic clove, crushed
4 pieces shin of veal, each about
5cm/2in thick
flour, for dredging
250ml/8fl oz/1 cup dry white wine
300ml/½ pint/1¼ cups meat or
chicken stock
1 bay leaf
1 sprig fresh thyme, or ¼ tsp dried thyme
salt and ground black pepper

FOR THE GREMOLATA
1 small garlic clove
30ml/2 tbsp chopped fresh parsley
5ml/1 tsp chopped lemon rind
½ anchovy fillet (optional)

SERVES 4

1 Preheat the oven to 160°C/325°F/Gas 3. Heat the butter with the crushed garlic clove in a heavy casserole large enough for the meat to fit in one layer.

2 Dredge the veal lightly in flour. Add to the pan and brown on both sides. Season with salt and pepper.

3 Add the wine, and cook over a moderate heat for 3–4 minutes, turning the veal several times. Add the stock, bay leaf and thyme. Cover, and bake for 2 hours.

4 Meanwhile, prepare the gremolata by combining the garlic, parsley, lemon rind and anchovy, if using, on a board and chopping them very finely.

5 Remove the casserole from the oven. Taste the sauce for seasoning. Add the gremolata, and mix it well into the sauce. Return the casserole to the oven for a further 10 minutes, then serve.

PORK WITH GREMOLATA

The ever-popular gremolata dressing adds a hint of sharpness to this Italian pork dish. This version gains subtlety by using lime rind as well as lemon.

INGREDIENTS
30ml/2 tbsp olive oil
4 pork shoulder steaks, about
175g/6oz each
1 onion, chopped
2 garlic cloves, crushed
30ml/2 tbsp tomato purée
400g/14oz can chopped tomatoes
150ml/¼ pint/⅔ cup dry white wine
bunch of mixed fresh herbs
3 anchovy fillets, drained and chopped
salt and ground black pepper
salad, to serve

FOR THE GREMOLATA
45ml/3 tbsp chopped fresh parsley
grated rind of ½ lemon
grated rind of 1 lime
1 garlic clove, chopped

SERVES 4

1 Heat the oil in a large flameproof casserole, add the pork steaks and brown on both sides. Remove the steaks.

2 Add the onion to the casserole and cook until soft and beginning to brown. Add the garlic and cook for 1–2 minutes, then stir in the tomato purée, chopped tomatoes and wine. Add the bunch of mixed herbs. Bring to the boil, then boil rapidly for 3–4 minutes to reduce and thicken slightly.

3 Return the pork to the casserole, then cover and cook for about 30 minutes. Stir in the chopped anchovies.

4 Cover and cook for 15 minutes, or until the pork is tender. Meanwhile, to make the gremolata, combine the parsley, lemon and lime rinds and garlic.

5 Remove the pork steaks and discard the bunch of herbs. Reduce the sauce over a high heat, if it is not already thick. Taste and adjust the seasoning.

6 Return the pork to the casserole, then sprinkle with the gremolata. Cover and cook for 5 minutes. Serve hot with a salad.

ROAST LAMB WITH HERBS AND GARLIC

This dish originates from southern Italy, where lamb is simply roasted spiked with slivers of garlic and wild herbs from the mountains.

INGREDIENTS

1.5kg/3–3½lb leg of lamb
45–60ml/3–4 tbsp olive oil
4 garlic cloves, halved
2 sprigs fresh sage, or pinch of dried sage
2 sprigs fresh rosemary, or 5ml/1 tsp
dried rosemary
2 bay leaves
2 sprigs fresh thyme, or 2.5ml/½ tsp
dried thyme
175ml/6fl oz/¾ cup dry white wine
salt and ground black pepper
fresh herbs, to garnish

SERVES 4–6

1 Trim any excess fat from the lamb. Rub with olive oil. Make small cuts in the skin all over the meat. Insert the garlic in some and a few of the fresh herbs in the others. (If using dried herbs, sprinkle on the meat.)

2 Place the remaining fresh herbs on the lamb, and allow it to stand in a cool place for at least 2 hours before cooking. Preheat the oven to 190°C/375°F/Gas 5.

3 Place the lamb in a large roasting tin, surrounded by the herbs. Pour on about 30ml/2 tbsp of the oil and season. Roast for 35 minutes, basting occasionally.

4 Pour the wine over the lamb. Roast for 15 minutes, or until cooked. Put the lamb on a heated serving dish. Tilt the tin, spooning off any fat on the surface. Strain the pan juices into a gravy boat. Slice the meat, and serve the pan juices separately, as a sauce. Garnish with fresh herbs.

KLEFTIKO

For this Greek speciality, marinated lamb steaks or chops are slow-cooked to develop an unbeatable, meltingly tender flavour. The dish is sealed with a flour dough lid to trap succulence and flavour, although a tight-fitting foil cover will serve equally well.

INGREDIENTS
juice of 1 lemon
15ml/1 tbsp chopped fresh oregano
4 lamb leg steaks or chump chops
with bones
30ml/2 tbsp olive oil
2 large onions, thinly sliced
2 bay leaves
150ml/¼ pint/⅔ cup dry white wine
225g/8oz/2 cups plain flour
salt and freshly ground black pepper
boiled potatoes, to serve (optional)

SERVES 4

COOK'S TIP
They are not absolutely essential for this dish, but lamb steaks or chops with bones will provide lots of additional flavour.

1 Mix together the lemon juice, oregano and salt and pepper, and brush over both sides of the lamb steaks or chops. Leave to marinate for at least 4 hours or overnight.

2 Preheat the oven to 160°C/325°F/Gas 3. Drain the lamb, reserving the marinade, and pat dry with kitchen paper. Heat the oil in a frying pan and fry the lamb over a high heat until browned on both sides.

3 Transfer the lamb to a shallow pie dish. Scatter the sliced onions and bay leaves around the lamb, then pour over the white wine and the reserved marinade.

4 Mix the flour with sufficient water to make a firm dough. Moisten the rim of the pie dish. Roll out the dough on a floured surface and use to cover the dish so that it is tightly sealed.

5 Bake for 2 hours, then break away the dough crust and serve the lamb hot, with boiled potatoes, if liked.

LAMB SAUSAGES WITH TOMATO SAUCE

he Greek name for these delicious sausages is *soudzoukakia*. They make a rich and tasty dish.

INGREDIENTS

50g/2oz/1 cup fresh breadcrumbs
150ml/¼ pint/⅔ cup milk
675g/1½ lb/6 cups minced lamb
30ml/2 tbsp grated onion
3 garlic cloves, crushed
10ml/2 tsp ground cumin
30ml/2 tbsp chopped fresh parsley
flour, for dusting
60ml/4 tbsp olive oil
salt and freshly ground black pepper
flat leaf parsley, to garnish

FOR THE SAUCE

600ml/1 pint/2½ cups passata
5ml/1 tsp sugar
2 bay leaves
1 small onion, peeled

SERVES 4

1 In a mixing bowl, combine the fresh breadcrumbs and the milk. Then add the minced lamb, onion, garlic, ground cumin and parsley and season with salt and ground black pepper.

2 Shape the lamb mixture with your hands into little fat sausages, about 5cm/2in long, and roll them in flour. Heat the olive oil in a frying pan.

3 Fry the sausages for about 8 minutes, turning them until evenly browned. Drain on kitchen paper.

4 Put the passata, sugar, bay leaves and whole onion in a pan and simmer for 20 minutes. Add the sausages and cook for 10 minutes. Take out the sausages and place on a serving dish, garnished with parsley.

COOK'S TIP
Passata is sieved tomato, which can be bought in cartons or jars.

LAMB FILO PIE

his recipe combines popular Greek ingredients: lamb and filo pastry. You can use chicken or fish too.

INGREDIENTS
sunflower oil, for brushing
450g/1lb/4 cups lean minced lamb
1 onion, sliced
1 garlic clove, crushed
400g/14oz can plum tomatoes
30ml/2 tbsp chopped fresh mint
5ml/1 tsp grated nutmeg
350g/12oz young spinach leaves
270g/10oz packet filo pastry
5ml/1 tsp sesame seeds
salt and freshly ground black pepper
salad or vegetables, to serve (optional)

SERVES 4

1 Preheat the oven to 200°C/400°F/Gas 6. Oil a 22cm/8½in round springform tin.

2 Fry the mince and onion without fat in a non-stick pan until golden. Add the garlic, tomatoes, mint, nutmeg and some seasoning. Bring to the boil whilst stirring, then simmer, stirring occasionally, until most of the liquid has evaporated.

3 Wash the spinach and remove any tough stalks, then cook in only the water clinging to the leaves for about 2 minutes, or until wilted.

4 Lightly brush each sheet of filo pastry with oil and lay in overlapping layers in the tin, leaving enough over-hanging to wrap over the top.

5 Spoon in the meat and spinach, then wrap the pastry over to enclose, scrunching it slightly. Sprinkle with sesame seeds and bake for about 25–30 minutes, or until golden and crisp. Serve hot, with salad or vegetables, if liked.

RABBIT SALMOREJO

R abbit is a popular meat in Spain. It makes an interesting alternative to chicken in this light, spicy sauté. Serve with a simply dressed salad.

INGREDIENTS
675g/1½lb rabbit portions
300ml/½ pint/1¼ cups dry white wine
15ml/1 tbsp sherry vinegar
several sprigs of fresh oregano
2 bay leaves
90ml/6 tbsp olive oil
175g/6oz baby onions, peeled and
left whole
1 red chilli, seeded and finely chopped
4 garlic cloves, sliced
10ml/2 tsp paprika
150ml/¼ pint/⅔ cup chicken stock
salt and ground black pepper
flat leaf parsley sprigs, to
garnish (optional)

SERVES 4

COOK'S TIP
If more convenient, transfer the stew to an ovenproof dish and bake at 180°C/350°F/Gas 4 for 50 minutes, or until the meat is tender.

1 Put the rabbit in a bowl. Add the wine, vinegar and herbs and toss together lightly. Cover and leave to marinate for several hours or overnight.

2 Drain the rabbit, reserving the marinade, and pat dry on kitchen paper. Heat the oil in a large sauté or frying pan. Add the rabbit and fry on all sides until golden. Drain well. Then fry the onions until just beginning to colour.

3 Remove the onions from the pan and add the chilli, garlic and paprika. Cook, stirring, for 1 minute. Add the reserved marinade, stock and a little seasoning.

4 Return the rabbit to the pan with the onions. Bring to the boil, reduce the heat and cover with a lid. Simmer very gently for about 45 minutes until the rabbit is tender. Serve the *salmorejo* garnished with sprigs of fresh parsley, if using.

BLACK BEAN STEW

T his simple stew uses a few robust ingredients to create a deliciously intense flavour – the Spanish equivalent of a French cassoulet.

INGREDIENTS

*275g/10oz/generous 1½ cups dried
black beans*
675g/1½lb boneless belly pork rashers
60ml/4 tbsp olive oil
350g/12oz baby onions
2 celery sticks, thinly sliced
10ml/2 tsp paprika
*150g/5oz chorizo sausage, cut
into chunks*
*600ml/1 pint/2½ cups light chicken or
vegetable stock*
*2 green peppers, seeded and cut into
large pieces*
salt and ground black pepper

SERVES 5–6

COOK'S TIP
This is the sort of stew to which you can add a variety of winter vegetables such as chunks of leek, turnip, celeriac and even little potatoes.

---

1 Put the beans in a bowl and cover with plenty of cold water. Leave to soak overnight. Drain the beans, place in a saucepan and cover with fresh water. Bring to the boil and boil rapidly for 10 minutes. Drain through a colander.

2 Preheat the oven to 160°C/325°F/Gas 3. Cut away any rind from the pork and cut the meat into large chunks.

3 Heat the oil in a large frying pan and fry the onions and celery for 3 minutes. Add the pork and fry for 5–10 minutes until the pork is browned all over.

4 Add the paprika and chorizo and fry for a further 2 minutes. Transfer to an ovenproof dish with the black beans and mix together well.

5 Add the stock to the pan and bring to the boil. Season lightly then pour over the meat and beans. Cover and bake in the oven for 1 hour.

6 Stir the green peppers into the stew, then cover and return to the oven for a further 15 minutes. Serve hot.

RICH BEEF CASEROLE

This full-bodied French dish should be served with mashed potatoes to absorb its delicious sauce. It is a perfect meal for a winter's day.

INGREDIENTS

1kg/2¼lb chuck steak, cut into cubes
2 onions, coarsely chopped
bouquet garni
6 black peppercorns
15ml/1 tbsp red wine vinegar
1 bottle full-bodied red wine
45–60ml/3–4 tbsp olive oil
3 celery sticks, thickly sliced
50g/2oz/½ cup plain flour
300ml/½ pint/1¼ cups beef stock
30ml/2 tbsp tomato purée
2 garlic cloves, crushed
175g/6oz chestnut mushrooms, halved
400g/14oz can artichoke hearts, drained and halved
chopped fresh parsley and thyme, to garnish
creamy mashed potatoes, to serve

SERVES 4

1 Place the meat cubes in a large bowl. Add the onions, bouquet garni, peppercorns, vinegar and red wine. Stir well, cover and leave to marinate overnight.

2 The next day, preheat the oven to 160°C/325°F/Gas 3. Using a slotted spoon, remove the meat cubes and onions from the marinade, reserving the marinade. Pat the meat and onions dry.

3 Heat the oil in a large flameproof casserole and fry the meat and onions in batches, adding a little more oil, if necessary. Remove and set aside.

4 Add the celery to the casserole and fry until lightly browned. Remove and set aside with the meat and onions.

5 Sprinkle the flour into the casserole and cook for 1 minute. Gradually add the reserved marinade and the stock, and bring to the boil, stirring. Return the meat, onions and celery to the casserole, then stir in the tomato purée and crushed garlic.

6 Cover the casserole and cook in the oven for about 2¼ hours. Stir in the chestnut mushrooms and artichokes, cover again and return to the oven for a further 15 minutes, until the meat is tender. Garnish with chopped parsley and thyme, and serve hot with creamy mashed potatoes.

PASTITSIO

 his Greek version of a pasta bake makes an excellent main meal – it is both economical and filling.

INGREDIENTS
15ml/1 tbsp oil
450g/1lb/4 cups minced lamb
1 onion, chopped
2 garlic cloves, crushed
30ml/2 tbsp tomato purée
25g/1oz/¼ cup plain flour
300ml/½ pint/1¼ cups lamb stock
2 large tomatoes
115g/4oz/1 cup pasta shapes
450g/1lb/2 cups Greek-style yogurt
2 eggs
salt and freshly ground black pepper
crisp salad and crusty bread, to serve

SERVES 4

1 Heat the oil in a large saucepan and fry the lamb for 5 minutes. Add the onion and garlic and fry for a further 5 minutes.

2 Stir in the tomato purée and flour. Cook for 1 minute.

3 Stir in the lamb stock and season with salt and pepper to taste. Bring to the boil and cook gently for about 20 minutes.

4 Slice the tomatoes, place the meat mixture in an ovenproof dish and arrange the tomatoes on top. Preheat the oven to 190°C/375°F/Gas 5.

5 Cook the pasta shapes in boiling salted water for 8–10 minutes or until just tender. Drain well.

6 Mix together the pasta, yogurt and eggs. Spoon on top of the tomatoes and cook in the preheated oven for 1 hour. Serve with a crisp salad and crusty bread.

PORK AND BEAN CASSEROLE

There are many versions of this classic dish, developed in the different regions of France. Some include goose and duck as well.

INGREDIENTS
30ml/2 tbsp olive oil
1 onion, chopped
2 garlic cloves, chopped
450g/1lb lean shoulder of pork, cubed
350g/12oz lean lamb (preferably leg), trimmed and cubed
225g/8oz coarse pork and garlic sausage, cut into chunks
400g/14oz can chopped tomatoes
30ml/2 tbsp red wine
15ml/1 tbsp tomato purée
bouquet garni
400g/14oz can cannellini beans, drained
50g/2oz/1 cup wholemeal breadcrumbs
salt and ground black pepper
salad and French bread, to serve

SERVES 4

COOK'S TIP
Replace the lamb with duck breast, if you like, but be sure to drain off any fat before sprinkling with the breadcrumbs.

1 Preheat the oven to 160°C/325°F/Gas 3. Heat the oil in a large flameproof casserole and fry the onion and garlic over a low heat until softened. Remove with a slotted spoon and reserve.

2 Add the pork, lamb and sausage cubes to the casserole, in batches if necessary, and fry over a high heat for a few minutes, stirring occasionally, until they are browned on all sides. Return the onion and garlic to the casserole and stir them into the meat.

3 Stir in the tomatoes, wine and tomato purée and add 300ml/½ pint/1¼ cups water. Season well and add the bouquet garni. Cover and bring to the boil, then transfer to the oven and cook for 1½ hours.

4 Remove the bouquet garni, stir in the beans and sprinkle the breadcrumbs over the top. Return the casserole to the oven, uncovered, for 30 minutes, until the top is golden brown. Serve hot with a green salad and French bread to mop up the juices.

MOUSSAKA

L ike many popular classics, a real moussaka bears little resemblance to the imitations served in Greek tourist resorts. This one is mildly spiced, moist but not dripping in grease, and encased in a golden baked crust.

INGREDIENTS
900g/2lb aubergines
120ml/4fl oz/½ cup olive oil
2 large tomatoes
2 large onions, sliced
450g/1lb minced lamb
1.5ml/¼ tsp ground cinnamon
1.5ml/¼ tsp ground allspice
30ml/2 tbsp tomato purée
45ml/3 tbsp chopped fresh parsley
120ml/4fl oz/½ cup dry white wine
salt and freshly ground black pepper

FOR THE SAUCE
50g/2oz/4 tbsp butter
50g/2oz/½ cup plain flour
600ml/1 pint/2½ cups milk
1.5ml/¼ tsp grated nutmeg
25g/1oz/⅓ cup grated Parmesan cheese
45ml/3 tbsp toasted breadcrumbs

SERVES 6

1 Cut the aubergines into 5mm/¼ in thick slices. Layer them in a colander, sprinkle with plenty of salt and leave for 30 minutes.

2 Rinse the aubergine slices in several changes of cold water. Squeeze gently with your fingers to remove the excess water, then pat them dry.

3 Heat some of the oil in a large frying pan. Fry the aubergine slices in batches until golden on both sides, adding oil if needed. Leave them to drain on kitchen paper.

4 Plunge the tomatoes into boiling water for 30 seconds, then refresh in cold water. Peel away the skins and chop roughly.

5 Preheat the oven to 180°C/350°F/Gas 4. Heat 30ml/2 tbsp olive oil in a saucepan. Add the onions and minced lamb and fry gently for 5 minutes, stirring and breaking up the lamb with a wooden spoon.

6 Add the chopped tomatoes, cinnamon, allspice, tomato purée, parsley, wine and pepper and bring to the boil. Reduce the heat, cover with a lid and simmer gently for 15 minutes.

7 Arrange alternate layers of the aubergine slices and meat mixture into a shallow ovenproof dish, finishing with aubergines.

8 To make the sauce, melt the butter in a small saucepan and stir in the flour. Cook, stirring, for 1 minute. Remove from the heat and gradually blend in the milk. Return the sauce to the heat and cook, stirring, for 2 minutes or until it thickens. Add the grated nutmeg, Parmesan cheese and some salt and pepper.

9 Pour the sauce over the aubergine slices and sprinkle with the toasted breadcrumbs. Bake for 45 minutes until golden and serve hot.

CASSEROLED RABBIT WITH THYME

T his is the sort of satisfying home cooking found in farmhouse kitchens and cosy neighbourhood restaurants throughout France, where rabbit is treated very much like chicken and enjoyed frequently.

INGREDIENTS
1.2kg/2½ lb rabbit
40g/1½ oz/¼ cup plain flour
15ml/1 tbsp butter
15ml/1 tbsp olive oil
250ml/8fl oz/1 cup red wine
350–475ml/12–16fl oz/1½–2 cups chicken stock
15ml/1 tbsp fresh thyme leaves, or
10ml/2 tsp dried thyme
1 bay leaf
2 garlic cloves, finely chopped
10–15ml/2–3 tsp Dijon mustard
salt and freshly ground black pepper
mashed potato, to serve

SERVES 4

1 Cut the rabbit into eight serving pieces. Chop the saddle in half and separate the back legs into two pieces each, leaving the front legs whole.

2 Put the flour in a polythene bag and season it with salt and black pepper. One at a time, drop the prepared rabbit pieces into the bag and shake well to coat them with flour. Tap off any excess, then discard any remaining flour.

3 Melt the butter with the oil over a medium-high heat in a large flameproof casserole. Add the rabbit pieces and cook until they are golden, turning them so that they colour evenly.

4 Add the wine and boil for 1 minute, then add enough of the stock just to cover the meat. Add the herbs and garlic, then cover and simmer gently for 1 hour, or until the rabbit pieces are very tender and the juices run clear when the thickest part of the meat is pierced with a knife.

5 Stir in the mustard, adjust the seasoning and strain the sauce. Arrange the rabbit pieces on a warmed serving platter with some sauce and mashed potato.

SKEWERED LAMB WITH CORIANDER YOGURT

Although lamb is the most commonly used meat for Greek and Turkish kebabs, chicken, lean beef or pork work equally well. For colour, you can add alternate pieces of pepper, lemon or onions, although this is not traditional.

INGREDIENTS

900g/2lb lean boneless lamb
1 large onion, grated
3 bay leaves
5 thyme or rosemary sprigs
grated rind and juice of 1 lemon
2.5ml/½ tsp caster sugar
75ml/5 tbsp/⅓ cup olive oil
salt and freshly ground black pepper
sprigs of rosemary, to garnish
grilled lemon wedges, to serve

FOR THE CORIANDER YOGURT

150ml/¼ pint/⅔ cup thick natural yogurt
15ml/1 tbsp chopped fresh mint
15ml/1 tbsp chopped fresh coriander
10ml/2 tsp grated onion

SERVES 4

1 To make the coriander yogurt, mix together the yogurt, mint, coriander and grated onion. Transfer the mixture to a small serving dish and refrigerate.

2 To make the kebabs, cut the lamb into 3cm/1¼in chunks and place in a mixing bowl. Mix together the grated onion, fresh herbs, lemon rind and juice, sugar and olive oil, then add salt and black pepper and pour over the lamb.

3 Mix the meat and its marinade together and leave to marinate in the fridge for several hours or overnight.

4 Preheat the grill. Drain the meat and thread it on to skewers. Arrange the kebabs on a grill rack and cook for about 10 minutes until browned, turning occasionally. Transfer to a plate and garnish with rosemary. Serve with the grilled lemon wedges and coriander yogurt.

PORK AND SAUSAGE CASSEROLE

A pork dish from Catalonia that uses the spicy *butifarra* sausage. This type of sausage can be found in some Spanish delicatessens but sweet Italian sausage will do.

INGREDIENTS
30ml/2 tbsp olive oil
4 boneless pork chops, about
175g/6oz each
4 butifarra or sweet Italian sausages
1 onion, chopped
2 cloves garlic, chopped
120ml/4fl oz/½ cup dry white wine
4 plum tomatoes, chopped
1 bay leaf
15ml/1 tbsp chopped fresh parsley
salt and ground black pepper

SERVES 4

1 Preheat the oven to 180°C/350°F/Gas 4. Heat the oil in a frying pan. Brown the pork chops on both sides (*left*), transfer to a plate and keep warm. Add the sausages, onion and garlic to the pan, cook until the sausages are browned and the onion is soft.

2 Stir in the wine, tomatoes and bay leaf, and season with salt and pepper. Add the parsley. Transfer to an ovenproof dish, cover, and bake for about 30 minutes. Slice the sausages, and serve immediately with the chops.

ROAST LOIN OF PORK STUFFED WITH FIGS, OLIVES AND ALMONDS

P ork is a popular meat in Spain and this recipe, using fruit and nuts in the stuffing, is of Catalan influence, where the combination of meat and fruit is quite common.

INGREDIENTS
60ml/4 tbsp olive oil
1 onion, finely chopped
2 cloves garlic, chopped
75g/3oz/1½ cups fresh breadcrumbs
4 ready-to-eat dried figs, chopped
8 green olives, stoned and chopped
25g/1oz/¼ cup flaked almonds
15ml/1 tbsp lemon juice
15ml/1 tbsp chopped fresh parsley
1 egg yolk
900g/2lb boned loin of pork
salt and freshly ground black pepper

SERVES 4

COOK'S TIP
Keep a tub of breadcrumbs in the freezer. They can be used frozen.

1 Preheat the oven to 200°C/400°F/Gas 6. Heat 45ml/3 tbsp of the oil in a pan, add the onion and garlic and cook gently until softened. Remove the pan from the heat and stir in the breadcrumbs, figs, chopped olives, flaked almonds, lemon juice, parsley and egg yolk. Season to taste.

2 Remove any string from the pork and unroll the belly flap, cutting away any excess fat or meat to enable you to do so. Spread half the stuffing over the flat piece and roll it up, starting from the thick side. Tie it at intervals with string.

3 Pour the remaining oil into a small roasting tin and place the pork in it. Roast the pork in the preheated oven for 1 hour 15–45 minutes, until cooked through. Shape the remaining stuffing mixture into even-size balls and add them to the roasting tin around the meat, 15–20 minutes before the end of the cooking time.

4 Remove the pork from the oven and let it rest for 10 minutes. Carve it into thick slices and serve with the stuffing balls and any juices from the tin. This dish is also good served cold.

LAMB STEWED WITH TOMATOES AND GARLIC

Take a train ride through the Tuscan countryside and you will often see sheep grazing alongside vineyards. This gloriously rustic stew celebrates both farming traditions.

INGREDIENTS
2 large garlic cloves
1 rosemary sprig or 45ml/3 tbsp chopped fresh parsley
60ml/4 tbsp extra virgin olive oil
1.2kg/2½lb stewing lamb, trimmed and cut into chunks
plain flour seasoned with ground black pepper, for dredging
175ml/6fl oz/¾ cup dry white wine
10ml/2 tsp salt
450g/1lb fresh tomatoes, chopped, or 400g/14oz can chopped tomatoes
120ml/4fl oz/½ cup hot lamb stock

SERVES 5–6

1 Preheat the oven to 180°C/350°F/Gas 4. Chop the garlic with the rosemary leaves or parsley. Heat the oil in a wide flameproof casserole.

2 Add the garlic with the rosemary or parsley, and cook over a medium heat, until the garlic is golden.

3 Toss the lamb in the seasoned flour. Add the lamb to the casserole and cook over a high heat until brown. Remove to a side plate, then pour the wine into the casserole.

4 Bring to the boil, scraping up any meat residues from the bottom. Return the lamb to the casserole and add the salt. Stir in the tomatoes and the stock. Cover the casserole, and bake for 1–2 hours.

BEEF STEW WITH RED WINE

Like much Tuscan cooking, this hearty stew is rustic in character. Serve it with mashed potatoes or pappardelle noodles.

INGREDIENTS

75ml/5 tbsp extra virgin olive oil
1.2kg/2½lb stewing beef, cut into
4cm/1½in cubes
1 onion, very finely sliced
2 carrots, chopped
45ml/3 tbsp finely chopped fresh parsley
1 garlic clove, chopped
2 bay leaves
few thyme sprigs, or
pinch of dried thyme
pinch of grated nutmeg
250ml/8fl oz/1 cup red wine
400g/14oz can chopped tomatoes
120ml/4fl oz/½ cup beef or chicken stock
15 black olives, stoned and halved
1 large red pepper, seeded and
cut into strips
salt and ground black pepper

SERVES 6

1 Preheat the oven to 180°C/350°F/Gas 4. Heat 45ml/3 tbsp of the oil in a large, heavy-based flameproof casserole. Brown the beef cubes, a few at a time, until coloured on all sides. Using a slotted spoon, transfer each successive batch to a plate.

2 Add the rest of the oil to the fat remaining in the casserole. When it is hot, cook the onion and carrots over a low heat for about 5 minutes or until the onion softens. Add the parsley and garlic and cook for 3–4 minutes more.

3 Return the meat to the pan, raise the heat, and stir well. Stir in the bay leaves, thyme and nutmeg. Add the wine, bring to the boil and cook, stirring, for 4–5 minutes. Stir in the tomatoes, stock and olives, mixing well. Season with salt and pepper. Cover the casserole and bake for 1½ hours.

4 Remove the casserole from the oven. Stir in the pepper strips. Return the casserole to the oven and cook, uncovered, for 30 minutes more, or until the beef is just tender, then serve.

Rice, Pasta and Pizza

Rice plays a leading role in the cooking of the Mediterranean region. It appears in the west as an accompaniment to kebabs and as a filling ingredient for stuffed vegetables, but most famously in delicious, creamy Italian risottos.

Pasta is the most important food in Italy, particularly in the south, where the "hard" durum wheat needed to make the best pasta is grown. Fresh pasta is now available in supermarkets, but the dried varieties are also excellent.

Pizza, another Italian speciality, can be as plain or elaborate as you like, topped simply with cheese and tomatoes, or with more substantial ingredients such as pepperoni and seafood.

RISOTTO WITH ASPARAGUS

 isotto is a popular Italian dish and this version is a good choice to make when asparagus is in season.

INGREDIENTS
225g/8oz fresh asparagus, lower stalks peeled
750ml/1¼ pints/3 cups vegetable or meat stock, preferably home-made
65g/2½oz/5 tbsp butter
1 small onion, finely chopped
400g/14oz/2 cups risotto rice, such as arborio
75g/3oz/¾ cup freshly grated Parmesan cheese
salt and freshly ground black pepper

SERVES 4–5

1 Bring a large saucepan of water to the boil and add the asparagus. Bring the water back to the boil, and blanch for about 5 minutes. Lift the asparagus out, reserving the cooking water. Rinse the asparagus under cold water and drain. Cut the asparagus diagonally into 4cm/1½in pieces. Keep the tip and next-highest sections separate from the stalk sections.

2 Place the vegetable or meat stock in a large saucepan, then measure out 900ml/1½ pints/3¾ cups of the asparagus cooking water, and add it to the stock in the pan. Heat the liquid to simmering and keep it hot until it is needed.

3 Heat two-thirds of the butter in a large heavy-based frying pan or casserole. Add the onion and cook until it is soft and golden. Stir in all the asparagus except the top two sections. Cook for 2–3 minutes. Add the rice, mixing well to coat it with butter, and cook for 1–2 minutes.

COOK'S TIP
Risottos have a distinctive creamy texture that is achieved by using arborio rice, a short-grain rice that absorbs plenty of stock, but retains its texture well.

---

4 Stir in half a ladleful of the hot liquid. Using a wooden spoon, stir constantly until the liquid has been absorbed or has evaporated. Add another half ladleful of the liquid, and stir again until it has been absorbed. Continue stirring and adding the liquid, a little at a time, for 10 minutes. Season to taste.

5 Add the remaining asparagus sections to the pan, and continue cooking, stirring and adding the liquid until the rice is tender but still firm to the bite. The total cooking time of the risotto may take from about 20–30 minutes and the amount of liquid needed may vary slightly.

6 Remove the risotto pan from the heat and carefully stir in the remaining butter and the Parmesan cheese. Grind in a little fresh black pepper, and taste once more before adding salt. Serve at once.

SPANISH SEAFOOD PAELLA

Paella is probably Spain's most famous dish. This recipe creates a delicious and wholesome seafood main course dish.

INGREDIENTS
60ml/4 tbsp olive oil
225g/8oz monkfish or cod, skinned and cut into chunks
3 prepared baby squid, body cut into rings and tentacles chopped
1 red mullet, filleted, skinned and cut into chunks (optional)
1 onion, chopped
3 garlic cloves, finely chopped
1 red pepper, seeded and sliced
4 tomatoes, skinned and chopped
225g/8oz/1¼ cups arborio rice
450ml/¾ pint/1⅞ cups fish stock
150ml/¼ pint/⅔ cup white wine
75g/3oz/¾ cup frozen peas
4–5 saffron strands, steeped in 30ml/2 tbsp hot water
115g/4oz/1 cup cooked, peeled prawns
8 fresh mussels in shells, scrubbed
salt and freshly ground black pepper
15ml/1 tbsp chopped fresh parsley, to garnish
lemon wedges, to serve

SERVES 4

1 Heat 30ml/2 tbsp of the olive oil in a large frying pan and add the fish and squid to the pan. Stir-fry for 2 minutes, then transfer to a mixing bowl with all the juices and reserve till needed.

2 Heat the remaining 30ml/2 tbsp of olive oil in the frying pan and add the chopped onion, garlic and red pepper. Fry for about 6–7 minutes, stirring frequently, until the onions and peppers have softened.

3 Stir in the chopped tomatoes and fry for 2 minutes, then add the arborio rice, stirring to coat the grains with oil, and cook for 2–3 minutes. Pour on the fish stock and wine and add the peas, saffron and water. Season well and mix.

4 Gently stir in the reserved cooked fish, with all the juices, and the prawns.

5 Having made sure that the mussels are clean and free of sand by scrubbing and rinsing in several changes of water, push them into the rice. Cover and cook over a gentle heat for about 30 minutes, or until the stock has been absorbed but the mixture is still moist.

6 Remove from the heat, keep covered and leave to stand for 5 minutes. Sprinkle with parsley and serve with lemon wedges.

GREEK STUFFED VEGETABLES

V egetables such as peppers make wonderful containers for savoury fillings. Instead of sticking to one type of vegetable, follow the Greeks' example and serve an interesting selection. Thick, creamy Greek-style yogurt is the ideal accompaniment for this dish.

INGREDIENTS
1 aubergine
1 large green pepper
2 large tomatoes
1 large onion, chopped
2 garlic cloves, crushed
45ml/3 tbsp olive oil
200g/7oz/1 cup brown rice
600ml/1 pint/2½ cups stock
75g/3oz/¾ cup pine nuts
50g/2oz/⅓ cup currants
45ml/3 tbsp fresh dill, chopped
45ml/3 tbsp fresh parsley, chopped
15ml/1 tbsp fresh mint, chopped
extra olive oil, to sprinkle
salt and freshly ground black pepper
Greek-style yogurt, to serve
fresh sprigs of dill, to garnish

SERVES 3–6

1 Halve the aubergine, scoop out the flesh with a sharp knife and chop it finely. Salt the insides well and leave to drain upside down for 20 minutes while you prepare the other ingredients.

2 Halve the pepper and seed and core it. Cut the tops from the tomatoes, scoop out the insides and chop roughly along with the tomato tops.

3 Fry the chopped onion, garlic and chopped aubergine in the olive oil for about 10 minutes, then stir in the rice and cook for 2 minutes more.

4 Add the tomato flesh, stock, pine nuts, currants and seasoning. Bring to the boil, cover and simmer for 15 minutes, then stir in the fresh herbs.

5 Blanch the aubergine and green pepper halves in boiling water for about 3 minutes, then drain them upside down.

6 Spoon the rice filling into all six vegetable "containers" and place them on a lightly greased ovenproof shallow dish.

7 Heat the oven to 190°C/375°F/Gas 5. Drizzle some olive oil over the vegetables and bake them for 25–30 minutes. Serve hot, topped with spoonfuls of Greek-style yogurt and garnished with dill sprigs.

PUMPKIN AND PISTACHIO RISOTTO

This elegant Italian risotto of creamy golden rice and orange pumpkin can be made as pale or bright as you like by adding different quantities of saffron.

INGREDIENTS
1.2 litres/2 pints/5 cups vegetable stock
or water
generous pinch of saffron thread
30ml/2 tbsp olive oil
1 onion, chopped
2 garlic cloves, crushed
450g/1lb arborio rice
900g/2lb pumpkin, peeled, seeded and
cut into 2cm/³⁄₄in cubes
175ml/6fl oz/³⁄₄ cup dry white wine
15g/¹⁄₂oz Parmesan cheese, finely grated
50g/2oz/¹⁄₂ cup pistachios
45ml/3 tbsp chopped fresh marjoram or
oregano, plus extra leaves, to garnish
freshly grated nutmeg
salt and ground black pepper

SERVES 4

COOK'S TIP
Italian arborio rice must be used for a true risotto. Choose unpolished white arborio as it contains more starch.

---

1 Bring the stock or water to the boil, then reduce to a low simmer. Ladle a little stock into a small bowl. Add the saffron threads and leave to infuse.

2 Heat the oil in a large saucepan. Add the onion and garlic and cook gently for 5 minutes until softened. Add the rice and pumpkin and cook for a few minutes longer until the rice looks transparent.

3 Pour in the wine and allow it to bubble fiercely. When the wine is absorbed add about a quarter of the stock and the infused saffron liquid. Stir constantly until all the liquid is absorbed.

4 Gradually add the remaining stock or water, a ladleful at a time, allowing the rice to absorb all the liquid before adding more, and stirring all the time. After 20–30 minutes the rice should be golden yellow and creamy, and *al dente* when tested.

5 Remove the pan from the heat and stir in the Parmesan cheese. Cover the pan and leave the risotto to stand for 5 minutes.

6 To finish the risotto, stir in the pistachios and chopped marjoram or oregano. Season to taste with a little nutmeg, salt and pepper, and scatter over a few extra marjoram or oregano leaves as a garnish, before serving.

SPAGHETTI WITH GARLIC AND OIL

This is one of the simplest and most satisfying pasta dishes of all. It is very popular throughout Tuscany.

INGREDIENTS
400g/14oz spaghetti
90ml/6 tbsp extra virgin olive oil
3 garlic cloves, chopped
60ml/4 tbsp chopped fresh parsley
salt and ground black pepper
freshly grated Parmesan cheese,
to serve (optional)

SERVES 4

1 Cook the spaghetti in a large saucepan of rapidly boiling salted water for 12 minutes, or for the amount of time suggested on the packet.

2 Meanwhile, heat the oil in a large frying pan and gently sauté the garlic until it is barely golden. Do not let it brown or it will taste bitter. Stir in the chopped parsley. Season with salt and pepper, then remove the pan from the heat.

3 As soon as the pasta is *al dente*, tip it into the frying pan with the oil and garlic. Return the pan to the heat and cook for 2–3 minutes, tossing the spaghetti to coat it with the sauce. Serve at once in a warmed serving bowl, with Parmesan, if using.

RAVIOLI WITH WALNUT AND CHEESE FILLING

Here home-made pasta is filled with a classic Italian combination of walnuts and cheese. It may be served on its own or with a sauce.

INGREDIENTS
200g/7oz/1½ cups strong plain flour
2.5ml/½ tsp salt
15ml/1 tbsp olive oil
2 eggs, beaten

FOR THE FILLING
1 small red onion, finely chopped
1 small green pepper, finely chopped
1 carrot, coarsely grated
15ml/1 tbsp olive oil
50g/2oz/½ cup walnuts, chopped
115g/4oz ricotta cheese
30ml/2 tbsp freshly grated Parmesan or Pecorino cheese
15ml/1 tbsp chopped fresh marjoram
salt and ground black pepper
extra oil or melted butter, to serve
fresh basil sprigs, to garnish

SERVES 6

1 Sift the flour and salt into a food processor. With the machine running, trickle in the oil and eggs and blend to a stiff but smooth dough. Allow the machine to run for at least 1 minute if possible, otherwise remove the dough and knead by hand on a lightly floured surface for 5 minutes.

2 If using a pasta machine, break off small balls of dough and then feed them several times through the rollers.

3 If rolling by hand, divide the dough into two and roll out each piece on a lightly floured surface to a thickness of about 5mm/¼in using a rolling pin. Fold each piece of pasta into three and re-roll. Repeat this process up to six times until the dough is smooth and no longer sticky. Roll the pasta slightly more thinly each time.

4 Keep the rolled dough under clean, dry dish towels while you complete the rest and make the filling. You should aim to have an even number of pasta sheets, all the same size if rolling by machine.

5 To make the filling, fry the onion, pepper and carrot in the oil for 5 minutes, then allow to cool. Mix with the walnuts, cheeses, marjoram and seasoning.

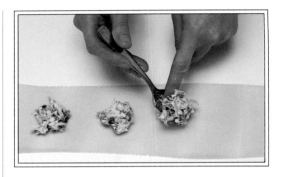

6 Lay a pasta sheet on a lightly floured surface and place small scoops of the filling in neat rows about 5cm/2in apart. Brush in between with a little water and then place another pasta sheet on the top.

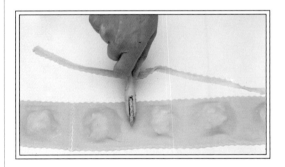

7 Press down well in between the rows then, using a ravioli or pastry cutter, cut into squares. Press the edges gently together with your fingers. Leave the ravioli in the fridge until dry, then boil in plenty of lightly salted water for just 5 minutes. Toss in a little oil or melted butter before serving, garnished with basil sprigs.

CANNELLONI WITH CHICKEN AND MUSHROOMS

This is a lighter alternative to the classic Italian cannelloni. Fill with ricotta, onion and mushroom for a vegetarian version.

INGREDIENTS
450g/1lb boneless, skinless chicken breast, cooked
225g/8oz mushrooms
2 garlic cloves, crushed
30ml/2 tbsp chopped fresh parsley
15ml/1 tbsp chopped fresh tarragon
1 egg, beaten
fresh lemon juice
12–18 cannelloni tubes
600ml/1 pint/2½ cups Tomato Sauce
50g/2oz/½ cup freshly grated Parmesan cheese
salt and ground black pepper
fresh parsley sprigs, to garnish

SERVES 4–6

1 Preheat the oven to 200°C/400°F/Gas 6. Place the chicken in a food processor or blender and process until finely minced. Transfer to a bowl.

2 Place the mushrooms, garlic, parsley and tarragon in the food processor or blender and process until finely minced.

3 Beat the mushroom mixture into the minced chicken with the egg, salt and black pepper and lemon juice to taste.

4 If necessary, cook the cannelloni in plenty of salted boiling water according to the manufacturer's instructions. Drain well on a clean dish towel.

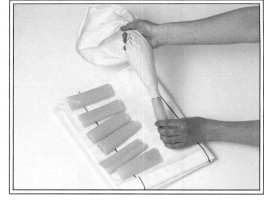

5 Place the filling in a piping bag fitted with a large plain nozzle. Use this to fill each tube of cannelloni.

6 Lay the filled cannelloni tightly together in a single layer in a buttered shallow ovenproof dish. Spoon over the tomato sauce so all the cannelloni are covered, and sprinkle evenly with the Parmesan cheese. Bake in the oven for 30 minutes or until browned and bubbling. Serve on warmed plates garnished with a parsley sprig.

PASTA WITH TOMATOES AND ROCKET

This pretty coloured pasta dish relies for its success on the salad green, rocket, which is commonly found in Italy as well as in other areas of the Mediterranean. Its delicious, slightly hot, peppery taste adds a surprising touch.

INGREDIENTS
450g/1lb pasta shells (conchiglie)
450g/1lb very ripe cherry tomatoes
75g/3oz fresh rocket
45ml/3 tbsp olive oil
salt and ground black pepper
Parmesan cheese, to serve

SERVES 4

1 Cook the pasta in plenty of boiling salted water according to the manufacturer's instructions. Drain well.

2 Halve the tomatoes. Trim, wash and dry the rocket.

3 Heat the oil in a large saucepan, add the halved tomatoes and cook them for barely 1 minute. The tomatoes should only just heat through and not disintegrate. Remove the pan from the heat.

4 Shave the Parmesan cheese using a rotary vegetable peeler.

5 Add the pasta, then the rocket, to the tomatoes. Carefully stir to mix and heat through. Season well with salt and freshly ground black pepper. Serve immediately with plenty of shaved Parmesan cheese.

PASTA WITH TUNA, CAPERS AND ANCHOVIES

This piquant sauce is typically Italian. It could be made without the addition of tomatoes – just heat the oil, add the other ingredients and heat through gently before tossing with the pasta.

INGREDIENTS
400g/14oz canned tuna fish in oil
30ml/2 tbsp olive oil
2 garlic cloves, crushed
750g/1¾lb canned chopped tomatoes
6 canned anchovy fillets, drained
30ml/2 tbsp capers in vinegar, drained
30ml/2 tbsp chopped fresh basil
450g/1lb garganelle, penne
or rigatoni
salt and ground black pepper
fresh basil sprigs, to garnish

SERVES 4

1 Drain the oil from the tuna into a saucepan, add the olive oil and heat gently until it stops "spitting".

2 Add the garlic to the pan and fry over a gentle heat, stirring, until golden. Stir in the tomatoes and simmer for 25 minutes, until thickened.

3 Flake the tuna and cut the anchovies in half. Stir into the sauce *(left)* with the capers and chopped basil. Season well.

4 Cook the pasta in plenty of boiling salted water according to the manufacturer's instructions. Drain well and toss with the sauce. Garnish with fresh basil sprigs.

BAKED LASAGNE

This is the classic Italian lasagne – rich meat and lightly spiced béchamel sauces layered with pasta sheets and Parmesan cheese.

INGREDIENTS
450g/1lb no pre-cook lasagne
115g/4oz/1 cup grated Parmesan cheese
25g/1oz butter

FOR THE BOLOGNESE SAUCE
60ml/4 tbsp olive oil
1 onion, finely chopped
2 streaky bacon rashers, chopped
1 carrot, finely chopped
1 celery stalk, finely chopped
1 garlic clove, crushed
350g/12oz minced beef
350ml/12fl oz/1½ cups red wine
400g/14oz can chopped tomatoes
1 bay leaf

FOR THE BECHAMEL SAUCE
750ml/1¼ pints/3⅔ cups milk
1 bay leaf
3 mace blades
115g/4oz/½ cup butter
75g/3oz/¾ cup plain flour
salt and ground black pepper

SERVES 8–10

1 First make the Bolognese sauce, heat the oil in a heavy saucepan, add the onion and cook over a gentle heat for 5 minutes. Add the bacon, carrot, celery and garlic and cook for 2–3 minutes more.

2 Stir in the minced beef and cook until browned. Add the wine, tomatoes and bay leaf and season to taste. Bring to the boil, then reduce the heat and simmer gently for 45 minutes.

3 Meanwhile, make the béchamel sauce. Heat the milk with the bay leaf and mace until almost boiling, then leave to stand for 15 minutes. Melt the butter in a pan, stir in the flour and cook for 1 minute. Strain in the milk, whisking all the time, bring to the boil, still whisking, and cook until thickened. Season to taste.

VARIATION
Reduce the amount of beef in the Bolognese sauce by 115g/4oz and add 115g/4oz sliced mushrooms with the wine and tomatoes instead.

4 Preheat the oven to 200°C/400°F/Gas 6. Spread a little Bolognese sauce in an ovenproof dish. Arrange two or three sheets of lasagne on top, cover with Bolognese sauce and then béchamel, then sprinkle with a little of the Parmesan.

5 Repeat the layers, ending with a layer of béchamel sauce. Sprinkle with Parmesan and dot with butter. Bake for 20–30 minutes until well browned and bubbling. Leave to stand for 5 minutes, then serve hot.

TAGLIATELLE WITH GORGONZOLA

G orgonzola is a mild creamy blue-veined cheese from Lombardy in northern Italy. As an alternative you could use Danish blue.

INGREDIENTS

25g/1oz/2 tbsp butter, plus extra for tossing the pasta
225g/8oz Gorgonzola cheese, crumbled
150ml/¼ pint/⅔ cup double or whipping cream
30ml/2 tbsp dry vermouth
5ml/1 tsp cornflour
15ml/1 tbsp chopped fresh sage
450g/1lb tagliatelle
salt and ground black pepper

SERVES 4

1 Melt the butter in a heavy-based saucepan. Stir in 175g/6oz of the crumbled Gorgonzola cheese and cook, stirring over a very gentle heat for 2–3 minutes until the cheese is melted.

2 Pour in the cream, vermouth and cornflour, whisking well to amalgamate. Stir in the chopped sage, then taste for seasoning. Cook, whisking all the time, until the sauce boils and thickens. Set aside.

3 Cook the tagliatelle in plenty of boiling, salted water for about 10 minutes. Drain thoroughly and toss with a little butter.

4 Reheat the sauce gently, whisking well *(right)*. Divide the pasta among four warmed serving bowls, top with the sauce and sprinkle over the remaining cheese. Serve immediately.

FETTUCCINE WITH PARMESAN AND CREAM

A classic dish from Rome, this is simply pasta tossed with double cream, butter, nutmeg and freshly grated Parmesan cheese. Popular but less traditional additions are tiny green peas and thin strips of ham.

INGREDIENTS
25g/1oz/2 tbsp butter
150ml/¼ pint/⅔ cup double cream, plus
60ml/4 tbsp extra
450g/1lb fettuccine
50g/2oz/½ cup freshly grated Parmesan
cheese, plus extra to serve
freshly grated nutmeg
salt and ground black pepper
dill sprigs, to garnish

SERVES 4

1 Place the butter and double cream in a heavy-based saucepan, bring to the boil and simmer for 1 minute until the mixture is slightly thickened. Remove the pan from the heat and set aside.

2 Cook the fettuccine in plenty of boiling salted water according to the manufacturer's instructions, but for 2 minutes less than the time stated. The pasta should still be a little firm.

3 Drain the pasta thoroughly and transfer to the pan with the cream sauce.

4 Return the pan to the heat and turn the pasta in the sauce to coat.

5 Add the remaining 4 tablespoons of double cream, the grated Parmesan cheese, salt and pepper to taste, and a little grated nutmeg. Toss until the pasta is thoroughly coated with the sauce and heated right through. Serve immediately from the pan and top with extra grated Parmesan cheese. Garnish with dill sprigs.

195

PASTA WITH TOMATO SAUCE

 his classic cooked Italian tomato sauce is simplicity itself – it goes well with almost any pasta shape.

INGREDIENTS
450g/1lb pasta, any variety
freshly grated Parmesan cheese, to serve

FOR THE TOMATO SAUCE
900g/2lb fresh ripe red tomatoes or
750g/1¾lb canned plum tomatoes
with juice
1 onion, chopped
1 carrot, diced
1 celery stick, diced
150ml/¼ pint/⅔ cup dry white
wine (optional)
1 fresh parsley sprig
pinch of sugar
15ml/1 tbsp chopped fresh oregano
salt and ground black pepper
fresh basil sprigs, to garnish

SERVES 4

COOK'S TIP
To stop pasta from sticking together
while it is boiling, add a little oil to the
cooking water first.

1 To make the tomato sauce, roughly chop the tomatoes, remove the cores, then place the tomatoes in a large saucepan.

2 Put all the remaining sauce ingredients, except the oregano, into the pan with the tomatoes, bring to the boil and simmer, half-covered, for 45 minutes until very thick, stirring occasionally. Pass through a sieve, or liquidize, then pour through a sieve to remove the tomato seeds. Stir in the chopped oregano. Taste for seasoning.

3 Cook the pasta in plenty of boiling salted water according to the manufacturer's instructions. Drain well.

4 Toss the pasta with the sauce. Serve with Parmesan, garnished with basil.

CALZONE

A speciality of the Apulia and Campania regions of Italy, calzone are simply pizzas with the topping on the inside.

INGREDIENTS
FOR THE PIZZA DOUGH
450g/1lb/4 cups plain flour
1 sachet easy-blend dried yeast
about 350ml/12fl oz/1½ cups warm water

FOR THE FILLING
5ml/1 tsp olive oil
1 red onion, thinly sliced
3 courgettes, sliced
2 large tomatoes, diced
150g/5oz mozzarella, diced
15ml/1 tbsp chopped fresh oregano
skimmed milk, to glaze
salt and ground black pepper
fresh oregano sprigs, to garnish

MAKES 4

COOK'S TIP
Don't add too much water to the dough when mixing otherwise it will be difficult to roll out – the dough should be soft, but not at all sticky.

1 To make the dough, sift the flour and a pinch of salt into a bowl and stir in the yeast. Stir in just enough warm water to mix to a soft but not sticky dough.

2 Knead for 5 minutes until smooth. Cover with clear film or a dish towel and leave in a warm place for about 1 hour, or until doubled in size.

3 Meanwhile, make the filling. Heat the oil and sauté the onion and courgettes for 3–4 minutes. Remove from the heat and add the tomatoes, mozzarella and oregano and season to taste with salt and pepper. Preheat the oven to 220°C/425°F/Gas 7 for at least 20 minutes.

4 Knead the dough lightly and divide into four. Roll out each piece on a lightly floured surface to a 20cm/8in round. Place a quarter of the filling on one half of each round. Brush the edges with milk. Fold over the filling. Press the edges firmly. Brush with milk. Bake for 15–20 minutes until golden. Garnish with oregano sprigs.

PEPPERONI PIZZA

S weet peppers, pepperoni and black olives make a glorious topping for this classic Italian pizza.

INGREDIENTS

FOR THE SAUCE

30ml/2 tbsp olive oil
1 onion, finely chopped
1 garlic clove, crushed
400g/14oz can chopped tomatoes
15ml/1 tbsp tomato purée

FOR THE PIZZA DOUGH

275g/10oz/2½ cups plain flour
2.5ml/½ tsp salt
5ml/1 tsp easy-blend dried yeast
about 175ml/6fl oz/¾ cup warm water
30ml/2 tbsp olive oil

FOR THE TOPPING

½ each red, yellow and green pepper,
sliced into rings
150g/5oz mozzarella, sliced
75g/3oz/½ cup thinly sliced pepperoni
8 black olives, stoned
3 sun-dried tomatoes in oil, chopped
2.5ml/½ tsp dried oregano
olive oil, for drizzling
fresh basil sprigs, to garnish

SERVES 4

1 To make the sauce, heat the oil in a pan, add the onion and garlic and fry gently for about 6 minutes. Stir in the tomatoes and the tomato purée. Bring to the boil and boil rapidly for 5 minutes. Remove from the heat and leave to cool.

2 For the pizza base, lightly grease a 30cm/12in round pizza tray. Sift the flour and salt into a bowl. Sprinkle over the yeast and make a well in the centre. Pour in the water and olive oil. Mix to a soft dough.

3 Knead the dough for 5–10 minutes, until smooth. Roll out to a 25cm/10in round, making the edges slightly thicker than the centre. Lift on to the pizza tray.

4 Preheat the oven to 220°C/425°F/Gas 7. Spread the sauce over the dough. Add the topping ingredients. Drizzle with oil. Cover loosely and leave in a warm place for 30 minutes.

5 Bake for 25–30 minutes and serve hot, garnished with a basil sprig.

SEAFOOD PIZZA

Any combination of shellfish or other seafood can be used as a pizza topping. Squid, mussels and prawns are classically Italian.

INGREDIENTS
*450g/1lb peeled plum tomatoes, fresh
or canned, weighed whole, without
extra juice
175g/6oz small squid
225g/8oz fresh mussels
1 quantity Pizza Dough (see page 199)
175g/6oz prawns, raw or cooked, peeled
and deveined
2 garlic cloves, finely chopped
45ml/3 tbsp chopped fresh parsley
45ml/3 tbsp olive oil
salt and ground black pepper*

SERVES 4

VARIATION
Fresh clams may be added: scrub well under cold running water. Heat in a saucepan until the shells open. Lift out and remove to a dish. Discard any that do not open. Break off the empty half shells, and discard. Add to the pizza after 8 minutes of baking.

1 Preheat the oven to 240°C/475°F/Gas 9 at least 20 minutes before baking the pizza. Strain the tomatoes through the medium holes of a food mill placed over a bowl, scraping in all the pulp.

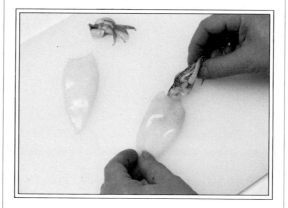

2 Working near the sink, clean the squid by first peeling off the thin skin from the body section. Rinse thoroughly. Pull the head and tentacles away from the body section. Some of the intestines will come away with the head.

3 Remove and discard the translucent quill and any remaining insides from the body. Sever the tentacles from the head. Discard the head and intestines. Remove the small hard beak from the base of the tentacles. Rinse the body and tentacles under running water. Drain. Slice the bodies into 5mm/¼in rings. Pat dry with kitchen paper.

4 Scrape any barnacles off the mussels, and scrub well with a stiff brush. Rinse in several changes of cold water. Place the mussels in a saucepan and heat until they open. Lift them out with a slotted spoon, and remove to a side dish. (Discard any that do not open.) Break off the empty half shells, and discard.

5 Roll out the dough to a 25cm/10in round. Spread some of the puréed tomatoes on it, leaving the rim uncovered. Dot with the prawns, squid rings and tentacles. Sprinkle with the garlic, parsley, salt and pepper, and olive oil. Immediately place the pizza in the oven. Bake for about 8 minutes.

6 Remove from the oven, and add the mussels in the half shells. Return to the oven and bake for a further 7–10 minutes, or until the crust is golden.

Breads

From Italian breadsticks to the olive breads of Greece, the Mediterranean region offers an intriguing variety of breads, many of which are now familiar worldwide.

Focaccia is a light, yeast-risen bread from Italy, made using olive oil, and often richly flavoured with olives, fruit, herbs or onions. Pizza bread is similar, and may be topped with a variety of flavourings or served simply as an accompaniment to a main meal.

Included in this chapter are some special-occasion breads – Greek Easter bread, olive and oregano bread, and bread with grapes. The other breads make good accompaniments, or may be sliced and served French-style, sprinkled over a bowl of steaming soup.

GREEK EASTER BREAD

In Greece, Easter celebrations are very important, and involve much preparation in the kitchen. This bread, known as *tsoureki*, is sold in all the baker's shops, and is also made at home. It is traditionally decorated with red dyed eggs and looks very attractive on the table.

INGREDIENTS
25g/1oz fresh yeast
120ml/4fl oz/½ cup warm milk
675g/1½ lb/6 cups strong plain flour
2 eggs, beaten
2.5ml/½ tsp caraway seeds
15ml/1 tbsp caster sugar
15ml/1 tbsp brandy
50g/2oz/4 tbsp butter, melted
1 egg white, beaten
2–3 hard-boiled eggs, dyed red
50g/2oz/½ cup split almonds

MAKES 1 LOAF

COOK'S TIP
You can often buy fresh yeast from baker's shops. It should be pale cream in colour with a firm but crumbly texture.

1 Crumble the yeast into a bowl. Mix with 15–30ml/1–2 tbsp warm water until softened. Add the milk and 115g/4oz/1 cup of the flour. Mix, cover with a dish towel, and leave for 1 hour in a warm place.

2 Sift the remaining flour into a large bowl and make a well in the centre. Pour in the risen yeast and draw in a little of the flour. Add the eggs, caraway seeds, sugar, brandy and remaining flour to form a dough.

3 Mix in the melted butter. Turn on to a floured surface, and knead for about 10 minutes, until the dough becomes smooth. Return to the bowl, and cover with a dish towel. Leave in a warm place for about 3 hours to allow the dough to rise.

4 Preheat the oven to 180°C/350°F/Gas 4. Knock back the dough, turn it on to a floured surface and knead for 1–2 minutes. Divide the dough into three, and roll each piece into a long sausage. Make a plait as shown above, and place the loaf on a greased baking sheet.

5 Tuck the ends under, brush with the egg white and decorate with the eggs and split almonds. Bake for about 1 hour, until the loaf sounds hollow when tapped on the bottom. Cool on a wire rack and enjoy with your meal or even for breakfast with coffee.

ITALIAN BREAD STICKS

These typically Italian bread sticks are especially delicious when hand-made. They are still sold loose in many bakeries in Turin and northern Italy.

INGREDIENTS
15g/½oz/1½ tbsp fresh cake yeast or
7g/¼oz/1½ tbsp active dried yeast
120ml/4fl oz/½ cup lukewarm water
pinch of sugar
5ml/1 tsp salt
200–225g/7–8oz/1¾ cups plain flour

MAKES ABOUT 30

1 Warm a mixing bowl by swirling some hot water in it, then drain. Put the yeast in the bowl, and pour on the warm water. Mix in the sugar, and allow to stand for about 10 minutes until the yeast starts to foam. Using a wooden spoon, mix in the salt and one-third of the flour. Mix in another third of the flour, stirring, until the dough forms a mass and pulls away from the sides of the bowl.

2 Sprinkle some of the remaining flour on to a work surface. Remove all the dough from the bowl and knead for 8–10 minutes, until the dough is smooth.

3 Tear a lump, the size of a small walnut, from the ball of dough. Roll it lightly between your hands into a small sausage shape. Set it aside on a lightly floured surface. Repeat until all the dough is used up and there are about 30 pieces.

4 Place one piece of dough at a time on a clean work surface without any flour on it. With both hands and your fingers spread, roll each piece of dough backwards and forwards into a long strand about 1cm/½in thick. Transfer to a lightly greased baking tray.

5 Preheat the oven to 200°C/400°F/Gas 6. Cover the tray with a cloth and leave the grissini in a warm place to rise for about 15 minutes while the oven is heating up.

6 Bake for 8–10 minutes, then remove from the oven. Turn the grissini over and put them back in the oven for 6–7 minutes more. Do not let them brown. Remove from the oven and allow to cool before serving. The grissini should be crisp when served. If they lose their crispness on a damp day, you can warm them in a moderate oven for a few minutes just before serving.

FOCACCIA

Very popular in northern Italy, focaccia is a form of flat bread that is oiled before baking. It is usually sold in bakeries cut into squares.

INGREDIENTS
275g/10oz/2½ cups plain flour
2.5ml/½ tsp salt
5ml/1 tsp easy-blend dried yeast
175ml/6fl oz/¾ cup warm water
30ml/2 tbsp olive oil
45ml/3 tbsp extra virgin olive oil
coarse sea salt

SERVES 6–8

1 Sift the flour, salt and yeast into a mixing bowl and make a well in the centre. Pour the water and olive oil into the well and mix to a soft dough. Knead for 5–10 minutes until smooth and elastic. Punch the dough down to remove any air.

2 Place the dough in a lightly oiled baking tin, then use your fingers to press it into an even layer 2cm/¾in thick.

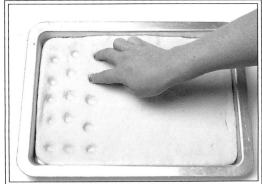

3 Cover the dough with a cloth and leave to rise in a warm place for 30 minutes. In the mean time, preheat the oven to 200°C/400°F/Gas 6. When the dough has risen, make light indents in the bread's surface using your fingers.

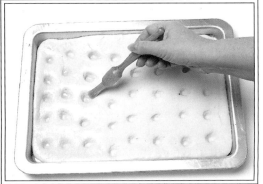

4 Brush the dough with the extra virgin oil, sprinkle with the salt and bake for about 25 minutes, or until just golden. Cut into squares or wedges and serve warm or at room temperature, as a side dish to a meal or as a snack on its own.

FOCACCIA WITH OLIVES

G reen olives make a classic topping for this Italian speciality – scatter over tiny fresh rosemary sprigs in place of the olives for a fragrant alternative.

INGREDIENTS
275g/10oz/2½ cups plain flour
2.5ml/½ tsp salt
5ml/1 tsp easy-blend dried yeast
175ml/6fl oz/¾ cup warm water
75ml/5 tbsp olive oil
10–12 large green olives, stoned and cut
in half lengthways
coarse sea salt

SERVES 6–8

1 Sift the flour, salt and yeast into a mixing bowl and make a well in the centre. Pour the water and 30ml/2 tbsp of the olive oil into the well and mix to a soft dough. Knead for 5–10 minutes until smooth and elastic. Brush a large round or square shallow baking tin with 15ml/1 tbsp of the remaining oil. Place the dough in the tin, and press it into an even layer 2cm/¾in thick.

2 Cover the dough with a cloth and leave for 30 minutes. Preheat the oven to 200°C/400°F/Gas 6. Make light holes in the bread's surface and brush with the oil.

3 Dot evenly with the olive pieces, and sprinkle with a little coarse salt. Bake for about 25 minutes, or until just golden. Cut into squares or wedges and serve warm or at room temperature, either as a side dish with a meal, or on its own.

BREAD WITH GRAPES

T his bread is made with wine grapes in central Italy to celebrate the grape harvest there.

INGREDIENTS

750g/1¾lb small black grapes
115g/4oz/½ cup sugar
275g/10oz/2½ cups plain flour
2.5ml/½ tsp salt
5ml/1 tsp easy-blend dried yeast
175ml/6fl oz/¾ cup warm water
30ml/2 tbsp olive oil
30ml/2 tbsp extra virgin olive oil

SERVES 6–8

1 Preheat the oven to 190°C/375°F/Gas 5. Remove the grapes from the stems, wash them and pat dry with kitchen paper. Place in a bowl and sprinkle with the sugar.

2 Sift the flour, salt and yeast into a bowl, make a well in the centre and pour in the water and olive oil. Mix to a soft dough, then knead for 5–10 minutes until smooth.

3 Divide the dough in half. Roll out each piece to a 20cm/8in round. Place one half on a lightly greased baking sheet and sprinkle with the sugared grapes.

4 Top with the second round of dough and crimp the edges together. Sprinkle the remaining grapes over the top. Cover loosely and leave to rise in warm place for about 30 minutes.

5 Drizzle the extra virgin olive oil over the bread and bake for 50–60 minutes. Allow to cool before cutting into wedges, then serve.

FOCACCIA WITH ONIONS

his appetizing Italian flatbread can be split and filled with prosciutto or cheese for an unusual sandwich.

INGREDIENTS
25g/1oz fresh yeast
400g/14oz/3½ cups strong
plain flour
10ml/2 tsp salt
105ml/7 tbsp olive oil
1 onion, sliced very thinly and cut
into short lengths
2.5ml/½ tsp fresh thyme leaves
coarse sea salt

SERVES 6–8 AS A SIDE DISH

1 Dissolve the yeast in 120ml/4fl oz/½cup warm water. Allow to stand for about 10 minutes. Sift the flour into a large bowl, make a well in the centre, and add the yeast, salt and 30ml/2 tbsp of the oil. Mix in the flour and add more water to make a dough.

2 Turn out on to a floured surface and knead the dough for about 10 minutes, until smooth and elastic. Return to the bowl, cover with a cloth, and leave to rise in a warm place for 2–2½ hours, until the dough has doubled in bulk.

3 Knock back the dough and knead again for 3–4 minutes. Brush a large shallow baking pan with 15ml/1 tbsp of the oil. Place the dough in the pan, and use your fingers to press it into an even layer 2.5cm/1in thick. Cover the dough with a cloth, and leave to rise in a warm place for 30 minutes.

4 Preheat the oven to 200°C/400°F/Gas 6. While the focaccia dough is rising, heat 45ml/3 tbsp of the oil in a medium frying pan. Add the onion, and cook over a low heat until soft. Stir in the thyme leaves.

5 Just before baking, use your fingers to press rows of light indentations into the surface of the focaccia. Brush with the remaining oil.

6 Spread the cooked onions evenly over the top of the flatbread and sprinkle lightly with some coarse salt. Bake the loaf for about 25 minutes, or until golden brown. Remove from the oven and cool slightly.

7 Cut the bread into squares or wedges and serve with a meal or on its own, either warm or at room temperature.

OLIVE BREAD

O live breads are popular all over the Mediterranean. For this Greek recipe, use rich oily olives or those marinated in herbs rather than canned ones.

INGREDIENTS

2 red onions, thinly sliced
30ml/2 tbsp olive oil
225g/8oz/1⅓ cups black or green olives, stoned
750g/1¾lb/7 cups strong plain flour
7.5ml/1½ tsp salt
20ml/4 tsp easy-blend dried yeast
45ml/3 tbsp each roughly chopped parsley and coriander or mint
feta cheese, to serve (optional)

MAKES 2 x 675G/1½LB LOAVES

1 Fry the onions in the oil until soft. Roughly chop the olives.

2 Put the flour, salt, yeast and parsley, coriander or mint in a large bowl with the olives and fried onions and pour in 475ml/16fl oz/2 cups hand-hot water.

3 Mix to a dough using a round-bladed knife, adding a little more water if the mixture feels dry.

4 Turn out on to a lightly floured surface and knead for about 10 minutes. Put in a clean bowl, cover with clear film and leave in a warm place until doubled in bulk.

5 Preheat the oven to 220°C/425°F/Gas 7. Lightly grease two baking sheets. Turn the dough on to a floured surface and cut it in half. Shape the dough into two rounds and place on the baking sheets. Cover loosely with lightly oiled clear film and leave until doubled in size.

6 Slash the tops of the loaves with a knife and then bake them for 40 minutes, or until the loaves sound hollow when tapped on the bottom. Transfer them to a wire rack to cool. Serve with feta cheese, if liked.

PIZZA WITH HERBS

hoose fresh "Italian" herbs, such as oregano, rosemary and basil, to top this Italian pizza bread.

INGREDIENTS
275g/10oz/2½ cups plain flour
2.5ml/½ tsp salt
5ml/1 tsp easy-blend dried yeast
175ml/6fl oz/¾ cup warm water
30ml/2 tbsp olive oil

FOR THE TOPPING
60ml/4 tbsp chopped mixed fresh herbs
coarse sea salt, to taste
90ml/6 tbsp extra virgin olive oil

SERVES 4

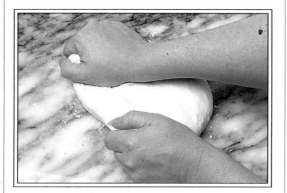

1 Sift the flour, salt and yeast into a bowl. Add the water and oil and mix to a soft dough. Knead for 5 minutes until smooth.

2 Lightly flour the work surface and then roll out the dough to a 25cm/10in round, making the edges of the round slightly thicker than the centre.

3 Transfer the round to a lightly oiled pizza tin or baking sheet, then pinch up the edges to form a shallow rim.

4 Sprinkle over the herbs and salt, and drizzle with the olive oil. Leave to rise in a warm place for 30 minutes. Preheat the oven to 240°C/475°F/Gas 9. Bake for 25–30 minutes, until golden. Serve immediately.

SESAME SEED BREAD

T oasted sesame seeds give this Greek bread its distinctive nutty flavour. The bread tastes good with savoury or sweet toppings.

INGREDIENTS
10ml/2 tsp dried yeast
pinch of sugar
175g/6oz/1½ cups plain flour
175g/6oz/1½ cups wholemeal flour
10ml/2 tsp salt
115g/4oz/½ cup toasted sesame seeds
milk, for glazing
25g/1oz/2 tbsp sesame seeds,
for sprinkling

MAKES 1 LOAF

1 Put 150ml/¼ pint/⅔ cup warm water in a jug. Sprinkle the yeast on top. Add the sugar, mix well and leave for 10 minutes.

2 Mix the flours and salt in a bowl. Make a well in the centre and pour in the yeast and 150ml/¼ pint/⅔ cup warm water.

3 With a wooden spoon, stir from the centre; incorporating flour with each turn, to obtain a rough dough.

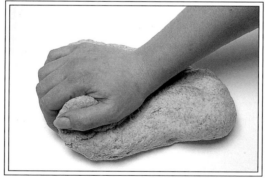

4 Transfer to a floured surface. To knead, push the dough away from you with the palm of your hand, then fold it towards you, and push away again. Repeat until smooth and elastic, return to the bowl and cover with a plastic bag. Leave in a warm place for 1½–2 hours until doubled in volume.

5 Grease a 23cm/9in cake tin. Punch down the dough and knead in the toasted sesame seeds.

6 Divide the dough into 17 balls and place in the prepared cake tin, making a loaf. Cover with a plastic bag and leave in a warm place until risen above the rim of the tin.

7 Preheat the oven to 220°C/425°F/Gas 7. Brush the top of the loaf with milk and sprinkle with the sesame seeds. Bake for 15 minutes. Lower the temperature to 190°C/375°F/Gas 5 and bake the loaf for about 30 minutes more until the bottom sounds hollow when lightly tapped. Cool on a wire rack, then serve.

OLIVE AND OREGANO BREAD

 This tasty Greek bread is an excellent accompaniment to all salads and it is particularly good served warm.

INGREDIENTS

5ml/1 tsp dried yeast
pinch of sugar
15ml/1 tbsp olive oil
1 onion, chopped
450g/1lb/4 cups strong white flour
5ml/1 tsp salt
1.5ml/¼ tsp freshly ground black pepper
50g/2oz/½ cup stoned black olives,
roughly chopped
15ml/1 tbsp black olive paste
15ml/1 tbsp chopped fresh oregano
15ml/1 tbsp chopped fresh parsley

MAKES 1 LOAF

1 Put 150ml/¼ pint/⅔ cup warm water in a jug. Sprinkle the yeast on top. Add the sugar, mix well and leave for 10 minutes.

2 Heat the olive oil in a frying pan and fry the onion until golden brown.

3 Sift the flour into a mixing bowl with the salt and pepper. Make a well in the centre. Add the yeast mixture, the fried onion (with the oil), the black olives, olive paste, herbs and 150ml/¼ pint/⅔ cup warm water. Gradually incorporate the flour and mix to a soft dough, adding a little extra water if necessary.

4 Turn the dough on to a floured work surface and knead for 5 minutes until it is smooth and elastic. Place in a mixing bowl, cover with a damp dish towel and leave in a warm place to rise for about 2 hours until doubled in bulk. Lightly grease a baking sheet.

5 Turn the dough on to a floured work surface and knead again for a few minutes. Shape into a 20cm/8in round and place on the prepared baking sheet. Using a sharp knife, make criss-cross cuts over the top, cover and leave in a warm place for 30 minutes until well risen. Preheat the oven to 220°C/425°F/Gas 7.

6 Dust the loaf with a little flour. Bake for 10 minutes, then lower the temperature to 200°C/400°F/Gas 6. Bake for 20 minutes more, or until the loaf sounds hollow when it is tapped lightly underneath. Transfer the bread to a wire rack to cool slightly before serving it.

Desserts and Cakes

Desserts in the Mediterranean range from a plate of fresh fruit served after a meal to elaborate pastries, such as honey and pine nut tart, and delicious Greek baklava, or rich chocolate and cream concoctions such as chocolate and chestnut roulade or the Italian tiramisù.

Many of the desserts in this chapter have become world-famous, including chocolate amaretti peaches, crema Catalana and the French classic pear and hazelnut flan. Also included are simple, refreshing desserts, such as fruit with yogurt and honey, figs with honey and wine, poached pears and red wine, and the ever-popular chocolate ice cream.

CHOCOLATE CHESTNUT ROULADE

This moist chocolate sponge has a soft, mousse-like texture as it contains no flour. Don't worry if it cracks as you roll it up. Chestnut purée is an important ingredient in French pâtisserie.

INGREDIENTS
175g/6oz plain chocolate
30ml/2 tbsp strong black coffee
5 eggs, separated
175g/6oz/¾ cup caster sugar
250ml/8fl oz/1 cup double cream
225g/8oz unsweetened chestnut purée
*45–60ml/3–4 tbsp icing sugar, plus extra
for dusting*
single cream, to serve

SERVES 8

1 Preheat the oven to 180°C/350°F/Gas 4. Line a 33 × 23cm/13 × 9in Swiss roll tin with non-stick greaseproof paper and brush lightly with oil.

2 Break the chocolate into a bowl and set over a saucepan of barely simmering water. Allow the chocolate to melt, then stir until smooth. Remove the bowl from the pan and stir in the coffee. Leave to cool slightly.

3 Whisk together the egg yolks and caster sugar in a separate bowl, until they are thick and light, then stir in the cooled chocolate mixture.

4 Whisk the egg whites in another bowl until they hold stiff peaks. Stir a spoonful into the chocolate mixture to lighten it, then gently fold in the rest.

5 Pour the mixture into the prepared tin, and gently spread with a rubber spatula to level the surface. Bake for 20 minutes. Remove the roulade from the oven, then cover with a clean dish towel and leave to cool in the tin for several hours, or overnight.

6 Put the double cream into a large bowl and whip until it forms soft peaks. In another bowl, mix together the chestnut purée and icing sugar until smooth, then fold into the whipped cream.

7 Lay a piece of greaseproof paper on the work surface and dust with icing sugar. Turn out the roulade on to the paper and carefully peel off the lining paper. Trim the sides. Gently spread the chestnut cream evenly over the roulade to within 2.5cm/1in of the edges.

8 Using the greaseproof paper to help you, carefully roll up the roulade as tightly and evenly as possible.

9 Chill the roulade for 2 hours, then sprinkle liberally with icing sugar. Serve in thick slices with a little single cream.

> ### COOK'S TIP
> Make sure that you whisk the egg yolks and sugar for at least 5 minutes to incorporate as much air as possible.

PEAR AND HAZELNUT FLAN

Fruit flans and tarts like this one are a feature of French pâtisserie. If you prefer, use ground almonds instead of the hazelnuts. If the filling mixture is a little thick, stir in some of the pear juice.

INGREDIENTS
115g/4oz/1 cup plain flour
115g/4oz/¾ cup wholemeal flour
115g/4oz/8 tbsp sunflower margarine
45ml/3 tbsp cold water

FOR THE FILLING
50g/2oz/½ cup self-raising flour
115g/4oz/1 cup ground hazelnuts
5ml/1 tsp vanilla essence
50g/2oz caster sugar
50g/2oz/4 tbsp butter, softened
2 eggs, beaten
45ml/3 tbsp raspberry jam
400g/14oz can pears in natural juice
a few chopped hazelnuts, to decorate

SERVES 6–8

1 Stir the flours together in a large mixing bowl, then rub in the margarine until the mixture resembles fine crumbs. Mix to a firm dough with the water.

2 Roll out the pastry and use it to line a 23–25cm/9–10in flan tin, pressing it firmly up the sides after trimming, so the pastry sits above the tin a little. Prick the base, line with greaseproof paper and fill with baking beans. Chill for 30 minutes.

3 Preheat the oven to 200°C/400°F/Gas 6. Place the flan tin on a baking sheet and bake for 20 minutes, removing the paper and beans for the last 5 minutes.

4 Meanwhile to make the filling, beat together all the ingredients except for the jam and pears.

5 Reduce the oven temperature to 180°C/350°F/Gas 4. Spread the jam on the pastry case base and spoon over the filling. Drain the pears well and arrange them, cut-side down, in the filling. Scatter with the nuts and bake for 30 minutes until golden brown and set.

TARTE TATIN

This delicious caramelized fruit tart was created by the Tatin sisters who ran a restaurant in Sologne in the Orléanais around the turn of the century.

INGREDIENTS
FOR THE PASTRY
50g/2oz/4 tbsp butter, softened
40g/1½ oz/3 tbsp caster sugar
1 egg
115g/4oz/1 cup plain flour
pinch of salt

FOR THE APPLE LAYER
75g/3oz/6 tbsp butter, softened
115g/4oz/generous ½ cup soft light brown sugar
10 firm eating apples, peeled, cored and thickly sliced
whipped cream, to serve

SERVES 4

1 To make the pastry, cream the butter and sugar in a bowl until pale and creamy. Beat in the egg, then sift in the flour and salt and mix to a soft dough. Knead the dough lightly on a floured surface, then wrap in clear film and chill for 1 hour.

2 Grease a 23cm/9in cake tin, then add 50g/2oz/4 tbsp of the butter. Place the cake tin on the burner and melt the butter gently. Remove and sprinkle with 65g/2½ oz/⅓ cup of the sugar.

3 Arrange the apple slices on top, then sprinkle with the remaining sugar and dot with the remaining butter.

4 Preheat the oven to 230°C/450°F/Gas 8. Place the cake tin on the burner again, over a low to medium heat, for about 15 minutes, until a light golden caramel forms on the bottom. Remove from the heat.

5 Roll out the pastry on a lightly floured surface to a round the same size as the tin and lay on top of the apples. Tuck the pastry edges round the sides of the apples.

6 Bake the tart for about 20–25 minutes, until the pastry is golden. Remove the tart from the oven and leave it to stand for about 5 minutes.

7 Place an upturned plate on top of the cake tin and, holding the two together with a dish towel, turn the apple tart out on to the plate. Serve the tart while still warm with whipped cream.

CHOCOLATE AMARETTI PEACHES

Quick and easy to prepare, this delicious dessert can also be made with fresh nectarines. Amaretti are Italian biscuits, similar to macaroons.

INGREDIENTS
115g/4oz amaretti biscuits, crushed
50g/2oz plain chocolate, chopped
grated rind of ½ orange
15ml/1 tbsp clear honey
1.5ml/¼ tsp ground cinnamon
1 egg white, lightly beaten
4 firm ripe peaches
150ml/¼ pint/⅔ cup white wine
15ml/1 tbsp caster sugar
whipped cream, to serve

SERVES 4

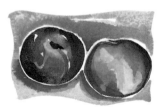

VARIATION
Omit the chocolate and increase the amaretti. Let the peaches cool, then serve on a bed of vanilla ice cream, accompanied by a raspberry sauce.

1 Preheat the oven to 190°C/375°F/Gas 5. Mix together the crushed amaretti biscuits, chocolate, orange rind, honey and cinnamon in a bowl. Add the beaten egg white and stir to bind the mixture.

2 Halve and stone the peaches and fill the cavities with the amaretti mixture, mounding it up slightly.

3 Arrange the stuffed peaches in a lightly buttered, shallow ovenproof dish which will just hold them comfortably. Pour the white wine into a measuring jug, then stir in the sugar.

4 Pour the wine mixture around the peaches. Bake for 30–40 minutes, until the peaches are tender. Spoon a little of the cooking juices over the peaches and serve with whipped cream.

APRICOT AND ALMOND JALOUSIE

J alousie means "shutter" in French, and the traditional slatted puff pastry topping of this fruit pie looks exactly like the shutters outside the windows of French houses.

INGREDIENTS
225g/8oz ready-made puff pastry
a little beaten egg
90ml/6 tbsp apricot preserve
30ml/2 tbsp caster sugar
30ml/2 tbsp flaked almonds
cream or natural yogurt, to serve

SERVES 4

1 Preheat the oven to 220°C/425°F/Gas 7. Roll out the pastry on a lightly floured surface and cut into a 30cm/12in square. Cut in half to make two rectangles.

2 Place one piece of pastry on a wetted baking sheet and brush all round the edges with beaten egg. Spread over the apricot preserve.

3 Fold the remaining rectangle in half lengthways and cut about eight diagonal slits from the centre fold to within about 1cm/½ in of the edge all the way along.

4 Unfold the pastry and place it on top of the preserve-covered pastry on the baking sheet, matching each edge carefully to the base. Press the pastry edges together well, to seal, and scallop the edges at close intervals with the back of a small knife.

5 Brush the slashed pastry top with a little water and sprinkle evenly with the sugar and the flaked almonds.

6 Bake in the oven for 25–30 minutes, until well risen and golden brown. Remove the jalousie from the oven and leave to cool on a wire rack. Serve the jalousie sliced, with cream or natural yogurt.

CREME CARAMEL

Of French origin, this creamy, caramel-flavoured custard now enjoys worldwide popularity. Do not put too much water into the roasting tin or it may bubble over into the ramekins.

INGREDIENTS
90g/3½ oz/½ cup granulated sugar
300ml/½ pint/1¼ cups milk
300ml/½ pint/1¼ cups single cream
6 eggs
90ml/6 tbsp caster sugar
2.5ml/½ tsp vanilla essence

SERVES 6

1 Preheat the oven to 150°C/300°F/Gas 2 and half fill a large, deep roasting tin with water. Set aside until needed.

2 To make the caramel topping, place the granulated sugar in a small saucepan with 60ml/4 tbsp water and heat it gently, swirling the pan from time to time, until dissolved. Increase the heat and boil, without stirring, to a good caramel colour.

3 Immediately pour the caramel into six ramekin dishes. Place the dishes in the roasting tin and set aside.

4 To make the egg custard, heat the milk and cream together in a pan until almost boiling. Meanwhile, beat together the eggs, caster sugar and vanilla essence.

5 Whisk the hot milk into the eggs and sugar, then pour the liquid through a sieve on to the cooled caramel bases.

6 Bake in the oven for 1½–2 hours (topping up the water level after about 1 hour), or until the custards have set in the centre. Lift out the dishes and leave to cool, then cover and chill overnight.

7 Loosen the sides of the chilled custards with a knife and invert on to serving plates, allowing the caramel sauce to run down the sides.

227

TIRAMISU

Tiramisu is Italian for "pick me up", and this rich egg and coffee dessert does just that! If you prefer, top with a sprinkling of grated chocolate instead of cocoa powder.

INGREDIENTS
500g/1¼lb mascarpone cheese
5 eggs, separated, at room temperature
90g/3½oz/½ cup caster sugar
pinch of salt
savoyard or sponge biscuits, to line dish(es)
120ml/4fl oz/½ cup strong espresso coffee
60ml/4 tbsp brandy or rum (optional)
unsweetened cocoa powder, to sprinkle

SERVES 6–8

1 Beat the mascarpone in a small bowl until soft. In a separate bowl beat the egg yolks with the sugar (reserving 15ml/1 tbsp) until the mixture is pale yellow and fluffy. Gradually beat in the softened mascarpone.

2 Using an electric beater or wire whisk, beat the egg whites with the salt until they form stiff peaks. Fold the egg whites into the mascarpone mixture.

3 Line one large or several individual dishes with a layer of biscuits. Pour the coffee into a measuring jug, add the reserved sugar, and stir in the brandy or rum, if using.

4 Sprinkle the coffee over the biscuits. They should be moist but not saturated. Cover with half the egg mixture. Make another layer of biscuits moistened with coffee, and cover with the remaining egg mixture. Sprinkle with cocoa powder. Cover, and chill in the fridge for at least 1 hour, preferably more, before serving.

ZABAGLIONE

In Italy, this airy egg custard fortified with sweet wine is usually eaten warm with biscuits or fruit. A small teaspoon of ground cinnamon may be added.

INGREDIENTS
3 egg yolks
45ml/3 tbsp caster sugar
75ml/5 tbsp marsala or white dessert wine
pinch of grated orange rind

SERVES 3–4

1 In the top half of a double boiler or in a bowl, away from the heat, whisk the egg yolks with the sugar until pale yellow. Beat in the marsala or wine.

2 Place the pan or bowl over a pan of simmering water, and continue whisking until the custard is frothy and evenly coats the back of a spoon, 6–8 minutes. Do not let the upper container touch the hot water, or the zabaglione may curdle.

3 Stir in the orange rind and serve the zabaglione immediately.

Tiramisu (left) and zabaglione (right)

CHURROS

These Spanish-style doughnuts are commercially deep fried in huge coils and broken off into smaller lengths for selling. Serve this home-made version freshly cooked with hot chocolate or strong coffee.

INGREDIENTS

200g/7oz/1¾ cups plain flour
1.5ml/¼ tsp salt
30ml/2 tbsp caster sugar
60ml/4 tbsp olive or sunflower oil
1 egg, beaten
caster sugar and ground cinnamon,
for dusting
oil, for deep frying

MAKES 12–15

1 Sift the flour, salt and sugar on to a plate or piece of paper. Heat 250ml/8fl oz/ 1 cup water in a saucepan with the oil until just boiling.

2 Tip in the flour and beat with a wooden spoon until the mixture forms a stiff paste. Leave to cool for 2 minutes.

3 Gradually beat in the egg until smooth. Oil a large baking sheet. Sprinkle plenty of sugar on to a plate and stir in a little ground cinnamon.

4 Put the dough in a large piping bag fitted with a 1cm/½in plain piping nozzle. Pipe little coils or S-shapes on to the prepared baking sheet.

5 Heat a 5cm/2in depth of oil in a large, deep-sided saucepan to 168°C/336°F, or until a little spare dough dropped in sizzles on the surface.

6 Using an oiled fish slice, lower several of the piped shapes into the oil and cook for about 2 minutes until light golden.

7 Drain on kitchen paper then coat with the sugar and cinnamon mixture. Keep warm. Cook the remainder in the same way and serve the *churros* immediately.

CREMA CATALANA

This delicious pudding from northern Spain is a cross between a *crème caramel* and a *crème brûlée*. It is not as rich as a *crème brûlée* but has a similar caramelized sugar topping.

INGREDIENTS
475ml/16fl oz/2 cups milk
rind of ½ lemon
1 cinnamon stick
4 egg yolks
105ml/7 tbsp caster sugar
25ml/1½ tbsp cornflour
grated nutmeg, for sprinkling

SERVES 4

1 Put the milk in a pan with the lemon rind and cinnamon stick. Bring to the boil and simmer for 10 minutes then remove the rind and cinnamon. Whisk the egg yolks and 45ml/3 tbsp of the sugar until pale yellow. Add the cornflour and mix well.

2 Stir in a few tablespoons of the hot milk, then add this mixture to the remaining milk. Return to the heat and cook gently, stirring, for about 5 minutes, until thickened and smooth. Do not let it boil. There should be no cornflour taste.

3 Pour the custard mixture into four shallow ovenproof dishes, about 13cm/5in in diameter. Leave to cool completely, then chill in the fridge, overnight if possible, until firm.

4 Before serving, preheat a grill. Sprinkle each dish with 15ml/1 tbsp sugar and a little grated nutmeg. Place the puddings under the grill, on the highest shelf, and grill until the sugar caramelizes. This will only take a few seconds. Leave the puddings to cool for a few minutes before serving. (The caramelized topping will only stay hard for about 30 minutes.)

CHOCOLATE RAVIOLI WITH WHITE CHOCOLATE FILLING

This spectacular Italian dessert is made from sweet pasta, with cocoa powder added to the flour. The pasta packets contain a rich creamy filling.

INGREDIENTS
175g/6oz/1½ cups plain flour
pinch of salt
25g/1oz/¼ cup cocoa powder
30ml/2 tbsp icing sugar
2 large eggs
single cream and grated dark and white chocolate, to serve

FOR THE FILLING
175g/6oz white chocolate
350g/12oz/3 cups cream cheese
1 egg, plus 1 beaten egg to seal

SERVES 4

VARIATION
Use milk chocolate instead of white chocolate for the filling, and sprinkle the finished dish with grated milk chocolate.

---

1 Put the flour, salt, cocoa and icing sugar into a food processor, add the eggs, and process until the dough begins to come together. Tip out the dough and knead until smooth. Wrap and rest for 30 minutes.

2 To make the filling, break up the white chocolate into squares and melt it in a basin placed over a pan of barely simmering water. Cool slightly, then beat into the cream cheese with the egg. Spoon into a piping bag fitted with a plain nozzle.

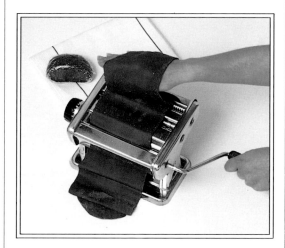

3 Cut the dough in half and wrap one portion in clear film. Roll out the pasta thinly to a rectangle on a lightly floured surface, or use a pasta machine. Cover with a clean, damp dish towel and repeat with the remaining pasta.

4 Pipe small mounds (about 5ml/1 tsp) of filling in even rows, spacing them at 4cm/1½in intervals, across one piece of the dough. Using a pastry brush, brush the spaces of dough between the mounds with beaten egg.

5 Using a rolling pin, lift the remaining sheet of pasta over the dough with the filling. Press down firmly between the pockets of filling, pushing out any trapped air. Cut into rounds with a serrated ravioli cutter or sharp knife. Transfer to a floured dish towel. Cover and rest for 1 hour.

6 Bring a large pan of water to the boil and add the ravioli a few at a time, stirring to prevent them sticking together. Simmer gently for 3–5 minutes, then remove with a slotted spoon. Serve with a generous splash of single cream and some grated chocolate.

ORANGE SORBET

Oranges were brought to Spain by the Arabs, and they are now one of Spain's most important crops. These little orange sorbets look very pretty served in the fruit shells.

INGREDIENTS
150g/5oz/¾ cup granulated sugar
juice of 1 lemon
14 oranges
8 fresh bay leaves, to decorate

SERVES 8

1 Put the sugar in a heavy-based pan. Add half the lemon juice and 120ml/4fl oz/½ cup water. Cook over a low heat until the sugar has dissolved. Bring to the boil and boil for 2–3 minutes, until the syrup is clear. Leave to cool.

2 With a sharp knife, slice the tops off eight of the oranges, to make "hats" for the sorbets. Scoop out the flesh of the oranges into a bowl and reserve. Put the orange shells and "hats" on a tray and place in the freezer until needed.

3 Grate the rind of the remaining oranges and add to the syrup. Squeeze the juice from the oranges and the reserved flesh. There should be 750ml/1¼ pints/3 cups. (If necessary, make up with bought fresh orange juice, or squeeze another orange.)

4 Stir all the freshly squeezed orange juice and the rest of the lemon juice, plus 90ml/6 tbsp cold water, into the sugar syrup. Taste, and add more lemon juice or granulated sugar if you need to. Pour the mixture into a shallow, freezer-proof container and place in the freezer for 3 hours.

5 Turn the mixture into a bowl and beat with a whisk to break down the ice crystals. Return to the container and freeze for 4 hours, until firm but not solid. Pack the mixture into the orange shells, mounding it up, and set the "hats" on top.

6 Store the oranges in the freezer until ready to serve. Just before serving, push a skewer into the tops of the "hats" and insert a bay leaf into each one.

NEW YEAR CAKE

A coin wrapped in foil is baked into this Greek cake, known as *vasilopitta*, and tradition holds that good luck will come to the person who finds it.

INGREDIENTS
275g/10oz/2½ cups plain flour
10ml/2 tsp baking powder
50g/2oz/½ cup ground almonds
225g/8oz/1 cup butter, softened
175g/6oz/¾ cup caster sugar
4 eggs
150ml/¼ pint/⅔ cup fresh orange juice
50g/2oz/½ cup blanched almonds
15ml/1 tbsp sesame seeds

SERVES 8–10

1 Preheat the oven to 180°C/350°F/Gas 4. Grease a 23cm/9in square cake tin, line the base and sides with greaseproof paper and grease the paper.

2 Sift the flour and baking powder into a large mixing bowl and then stir in the ground almonds.

3 In another mixing bowl, cream together the butter and sugar until light and fluffy. Beat in the eggs, one at a time, using an electric mixer. Fold in the flour mixture, alternating with the orange juice, until evenly combined.

4 Add a coin wrapped in foil if you wish to make the cake in the traditional manner, then spoon the cake mixture into the prepared tin and smooth the surface. Arrange the almonds on top, then sprinkle over the sesame seeds. Bake in the centre of the oven for 50–55 minutes, or until a skewer inserted into the centre of the cake comes out clean. Leave to cool in the tin for about 5 minutes, then turn out on to a wire rack. Peel off the lining paper and leave the cake to cool completely. Serve cut into diamond shapes.

> COOK'S TIP
> This cake can be kept for up to 4 days in an airtight container.

HONEY AND LEMON CAKE

This tangy cake makes a perfect mid-afternoon snack. Honey is used to sweeten many Greek dishes, and it adds its wonderful flavour to this cake.

INGREDIENTS
150g/5oz/1¼ cups plain flour
7.5ml/1½ tsp baking powder
2.5ml/½ tsp grated nutmeg
50g/2oz/⅓ cup semolina
2 egg whites
40g/1½oz/3 tbsp butter
60ml/4 tbsp clear honey
finely grated rind and juice of 1 lemon
150ml/¼ pint/⅔ cup milk
10ml/2 tsp sesame seeds

MAKES 16 SLICES

1 Preheat the oven to 200°C/400°F/Gas 6. Lightly grease a 19cm/7½in square deep cake tin and line the base with non-stick baking paper.

2 Sift together the flour, baking powder and nutmeg in a bowl, then beat in the semolina. Whisk the egg whites until they form soft peaks, then fold them evenly into the cake mixture.

3 Place the butter and 45ml/3 tbsp of the clear honey in a saucepan and heat gently until melted. Put aside 15ml/1 tbsp of the lemon juice, then stir the rest in the honey mixture along with the lemon rind and milk. Stir into the flour mixture.

4 Spoon the cake mixture into the tin and sprinkle with sesame seeds. Bake for 25–30 minutes, until golden brown. Mix the reserved honey and lemon juice and drizzle over the cake while warm. Cool in the tin, then cut into fingers to serve.

LOUKOUMIA

This is the Greek version of Turkish Delight and this versatile recipe can be made in minutes. Serve a few cubes with coffee after a heavy meal, for a pick-me-up. You can put cocktail sticks in each piece and decorate with a sprinkling of icing sugar.

INGREDIENTS
400g/14oz/2 cups sugar
300ml/½ pint/1¼ cups water
25g/1oz powdered gelatine
2.5ml/½ tsp cream of tartar
30ml/2 tbsp rose water
pink food colouring
45ml/3 tbsp icing sugar, sifted
15ml/1 tbsp cornflour

MAKES 450G/1LB

VARIATION
Try different flavours in this recipe, such as lemon, crème de menthe and orange and then vary the food colouring accordingly. For a truly authentic touch, add some chopped pistachio nuts to the mixture before pouring into the tins.

1 Wet the insides of two 18cm/7in shallow square tins with water. Place the sugar and all but 60ml/4 tbsp of the water in a heavy-based saucepan. Heat gently, stirring occasionally, until the sugar has dissolved.

2 Blend the gelatine and remaining water in a small bowl and place in a saucepan of hot water. Stir occasionally until dissolved.

3 Bring the sugar syrup to the boil and boil steadily for about 8 minutes until the syrup registers 130°C/260°F on a sugar thermometer. Stir the cream of tartar into the gelatine, then pour into the boiling syrup and stir until well blended. Remove from the heat.

4 Add the rose water and a few drops of pink food colouring to tint the mixture pale pink. Pour the mixture into the tins and allow to set for several hours or overnight.

5 Dust a sheet of waxed or greaseproof paper with some of the sugar and cornflour. Dip the base of the tin in hot water. Invert on to the paper. Cut into 2.5cm/1in squares using an oiled knife. Toss in icing sugar to coat.

FRUIT WITH YOGURT AND HONEY

F resh fruit most commonly follows a meal in Greece, and the addition of yogurt and honey makes it even more delicious.

INGREDIENTS
225g/8oz/1 cup Greek-style yogurt
45ml/3 tbsp clear honey
selection of fresh fruit for dipping, such as apples, pears, tangerines, grapes, figs and strawberries

SERVES 4

1 Beat the yogurt, place in a dish, and stir in the honey, to leave a marbled effect.

2 Cut the fruits into wedges or bite-size pieces, or leave whole.

3 Arrange the fruits on a platter with the bowl of dip in the centre. Serve chilled.

FIGS WITH HONEY AND WINE

The best figs come from Greece and Turkey. Any variety can be used in this recipe; choose figs that are plump and firm, and use them quickly as they don't store well.

INGREDIENTS
450ml/¾ pint/scant 2 cups dry white wine
75g/3oz/⅓ cup clear honey
50g/2oz/¼ cup caster sugar
1 small orange
8 whole cloves
450g/1lb fresh figs
1 cinnamon stick
mint sprigs or bay leaves, to decorate

FOR THE CREAM
300ml/½ pint/1¼ cups double cream
1 vanilla pod
5ml/1 tsp caster sugar

SERVES 6

1 Put the wine, honey and sugar in a heavy-based saucepan and heat gently until the sugar dissolves.

2 Stud the orange with the cloves and add to the syrup with the figs and cinnamon. Cover and simmer gently for 5–10 minutes until the figs are softened. Transfer to a serving dish and leave to cool.

3 Put 150ml/¼ pint/⅔ cup of the cream in a small saucepan with the vanilla pod. Bring almost to the boil, then leave to cool and infuse for 30 minutes. Remove the vanilla pod and mix the flavoured cream with the remaining cream and sugar in a mixing bowl. Whip lightly. Transfer to a serving dish and serve with the figs.

BAKLAVA

his deliciously sticky pastry is popular all over Greece and across much of the Middle East.

INGREDIENTS
150g/5oz/⅔ cup unsalted butter, melted
350g/12oz/3 cups ground pistachio nuts
150g/5oz/1¼ cups icing sugar
15ml/1 tbsp ground cardamom
450g/1lb filo pastry

FOR THE SYRUP
450g/1lb/2¼ cups sugar
30ml/2 tbsp rose water

SERVES 6–8

1 For the syrup, heat 300ml/½ pint/1¼ cups water with the sugar in a saucepan.

2 Bring to the boil and simmer for about 10 minutes until syrupy. Stir in the rose water and leave to cool.

3 Preheat the oven to 160°C/325°F/Gas 3. Brush a large rectangular baking tin with a little melted butter.

4 Mix together the ground pistachio nuts, icing sugar and cardamom to make the filling mixture.

5 Taking one sheet of filo pastry at a time, and keeping the remainder covered with a damp dish towel, brush with melted butter and lay on the bottom of the tin. Continue until you have six buttered layers in the tin. Spread half of the nut mixture over, pressing down with a spoon.

6 Take another six sheets of filo pastry, brush with butter, one by one, and lay over the nut mixture. Sprinkle over the remaining nuts and top with a final layer of six filo sheets brushed again with butter. Cut the pastry diagonally into small lozenge shapes using a sharp knife. Pour the remaining melted butter over the top.

7 Bake the pastries for 20 minutes, then increase the heat to 200°C/400°F/Gas 6 and bake for 15 minutes until light golden.

8 Remove from the oven and drizzle about three-quarters of the syrup over the pastry, reserving the remainder for serving. Leave to cool overnight and re-cut the pieces. Arrange the Baklava lozenges on a large glass dish, and serve with extra syrup.

CHESTNUT PUDDING

I n Tuscany, chestnuts are gathered during late autumn and made into delicious puddings. This is one of the best in Italy.

INGREDIENTS
450g/1lb fresh chestnuts
300ml/½ pint/1¼ cups milk
115g/4oz/½ cup caster sugar
2 eggs, separated, at room temperature
25g/1oz/¼ cup cocoa powder
2.5ml/½ tsp vanilla essence
50g/2oz/scant ½ cup icing sugar, sifted
butter, for greasing
whipped cream and marrons glacés,
to decorate

SERVES 4–5

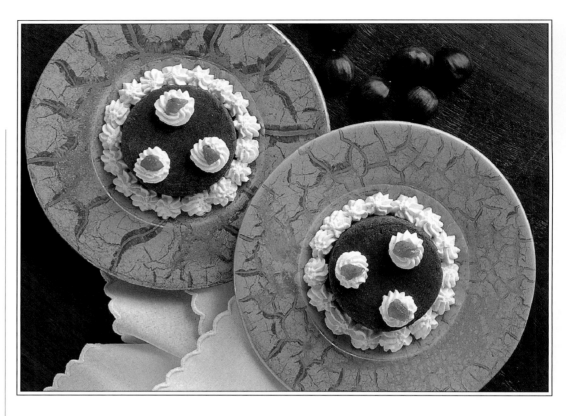

1 Preheat the oven to 180°C/350°F/Gas 4. Butter four individual pudding bowls. Cut a cross in the flat side of each chestnut. Cook the chestnuts in boiling water for 5–6 minutes. Remove with a slotted spoon, and peel off the skins while still warm.

2 Place the peeled chestnuts in a heavy-based or non-stick saucepan. Add the milk and half the caster sugar. Cook over a low heat, stirring occasionally, until soft. Allow to cool, then press the contents of the pan through a strainer into a clean bowl.

3 In a separate bowl, beat the egg yolks with the remaining caster sugar until the mixture is pale yellow and fluffy. Beat in the cocoa powder and the vanilla. Using a wire whisk or hand-held electric beater, whisk the egg whites until they form soft peaks. Beat in the sifted icing sugar. Continue beating until the mixture forms stiff peaks.

4 Fold the chestnut and egg yolk mixtures together, then the egg whites. Spoon into the greased bowls. Place on a baking sheet and bake for 15–20 minutes. Cool for 10 minutes before turning the puddings out. Pipe with whipped cream and decorate with marrons glacés.

POACHED PEARS IN RED WINE

INGREDIENTS
1 bottle red wine
150g/5oz/⅔ cup caster sugar
45ml/3 tbsp clear honey
juice of ½ lemon
1 cinnamon stick
1 vanilla pod, split open lengthways
5cm/2in piece of orange rind
1 clove
1 black peppercorn
4 firm ripe pears of similar size
whipped cream or soured cream, to serve

SERVES 4

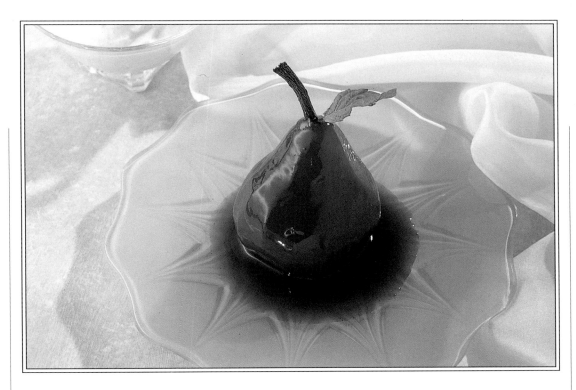

1 Place the red wine, caster sugar, honey, lemon juice, cinnamon stick, vanilla pod, orange rind, clove and peppercorn in a saucepan just large enough to hold the pears upright. Heat gently over a low heat, stirring occasionally, until the sugar has completely dissolved.

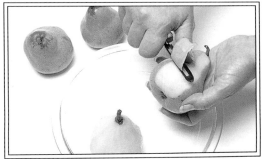

2 Meanwhile, peel the pears, leaving the stem on each intact. Take a thin slice off the base of each pear so that it will stand level on a serving dish.

3 Stand the pears upright in the wine mixture. Simmer, uncovered, for 20–35 minutes depending on size and ripeness, until the pears are just tender; be careful not to overcook. Test gently with the tip of a sharp knife.

4 Using a slotted spoon, carefully transfer the pears to a bowl. Continue to boil the poaching liquid until reduced by about half. Leave to cool, then strain the cooled liquid over the pears and chill for at least 3 hours.

5 Place each pear in an individual serving dish and spoon over a little of the red wine syrup. Serve with chilled whipped or soured cream.

CREPES SUZETTE

An impressive French dessert, ideal for serving at the end of a formal dinner party. For a special touch, flame the brandy as you pour it into the pan.

INGREDIENTS
FOR THE CREPES
115g/4oz/1 cup plain flour
pinch of salt
1 egg
1 egg yolk
300ml/½ pint/1¼ cups skimmed milk
15ml/1 tbsp unsalted butter, melted, plus extra for frying

FOR THE SAUCE
2 large oranges
50g/2oz/4 tbsp butter
115g/4oz/generous ½ cup soft light brown sugar
15ml/1 tbsp Grand Marnier
15ml/1 tbsp brandy

MAKES 8

1 Sift the flour and salt into a bowl and make a well in the centre. Add the egg and the extra yolk into the well. Stir with a wooden spoon to incorporate the flour from around the edges.

2 When the mixture thickens, gradually pour on the milk, beating well after each addition, until a smooth batter is formed. Stir in the butter, transfer to a measuring jug, cover and chill.

3 Heat a 20cm/8in shallow frying pan, add a little butter and heat until sizzling. Pour in a little of the batter, tilting the pan back and forth to cover the base thinly.

4 Cook the crepes over a medium heat for 1–2 minutes until lightly browned underneath, then flip over with a spatula and cook for 1 minute. Repeat this process until you have eight crêpes. Pile them up on a plate as they are ready.

5 Pare the rind from one of the oranges and reserve 5ml/1 tsp for decoration. Squeeze the juice from both oranges.

6 To make the sauce, melt the butter in a large frying pan and add the sugar, orange rind and juice. Heat gently until the sugar has dissolved and the mixture is bubbling. Fold each crêpe in quarters. Add to the pan one at a time, coat in the sauce and fold in half again. Push to the side of the pan to make room for the others.

7 Pour on the Grand Marnier and brandy and cook gently for 2–3 minutes, until the sauce has slightly caramelized. Serve, sprinkled with the reserved orange rind.

ORANGE RICE PUDDING

In Spain, Greece, Italy and Morocco rice puddings are a favourite dish, especially when sweetened with honey and flavoured with orange.

INGREDIENTS
50g/2oz/¼ cup short-grain pudding rice
600ml/1 pint/2½ cups milk
30–45ml/2–3 tbsp clear honey,
according to taste
finely grated rind of ½ small orange
150ml/¼ pint/⅔ cup double cream
15ml/1 tbsp chopped pistachio
nuts, toasted, to decorate

SERVES 4

1 Mix the rice with the milk, honey and orange rind in a saucepan and bring to the boil, then reduce the heat, cover and simmer very gently for about 1¼ hours, stirring regularly.

2 Remove the lid from the saucepan and continue cooking and stirring the mixture for about 15–20 minutes, or until the rice is creamy.

3 Pour in the double cream and simmer for 5–8 minutes longer. Serve the rice sprinkled with the pistachio nuts in individual warmed bowls, or serve chilled.

CHOCOLATE ICE CREAM

 talian ice cream is often said to be the best. Use good-quality chocolate in this classic *gelato* recipe.

INGREDIENTS
900ml/1½ pints/scant 3¾ cups milk
10cm/4in piece of vanilla pod
4 egg yolks
90g/3½oz/½ cup sugar
225g/8oz cooking chocolate, melted

MAKES ABOUT 3¾ CUPS

VARIATION
To make custard ice cream, replace the vanilla pod with 2.5 ml/½ tsp grated lemon zest, and use 6 egg yolks. Leave out the chocolate.

1 Make a custard by heating the milk with the vanilla pod in a small saucepan. Do not let the milk boil.

2 Beat the egg yolks with a wire whisk or electric beater. Gradually incorporate the sugar, and continue beating for 5 minutes, or until the mixture turns pale yellow. Strain the milk and slowly add it to the egg mixture gradually.

3 Pour the mixture and the chocolate into a bowl placed over a pan of simmering water. Stir over a moderate heat until the water in the pan is boiling, and the custard thickens to lightly coat the back of a spoon. Remove from the heat and allow to cool.

4 Freeze the chocolate ice cream in an ice cream maker, or place it in a freezer container. Freeze for 3 hours, chop and process, then return to the freezer. Repeat this process 2–3 times until a smooth consistency has been reached.

HALVA

The Greeks love home-made halva which they cook in a saucepan with semolina, olive oil, sugar, honey and almonds. You can either eat it warm, or allow it to set and then cut it into slices or squares.

INGREDIENTS
400g/14oz/2 cups sugar
1 litre/1¾ pints/4 cups water
2 cinnamon sticks
250ml/8fl oz/1 cup olive oil
350g/12oz/3 cups semolina
75g/3oz/¾ cup blanched almonds,
6–8 halved, the rest chopped
120ml/4fl oz/½ cup clear honey
ground cinnamon, to serve

MAKES 12–16 PIECES

1 Reserve 2oz/¼ cup of the sugar and dissolve the rest in the water over a gentle heat, stirring from time to time.

2 Add the cinnamon sticks, bring to the boil, then simmer for 5 minutes. Cool and remove the cinnamon sticks.

3 Heat the olive oil in a heavy-based saucepan and, when it is quite hot, stir in the semolina. Cook, stirring occasionally, until it turns golden brown, then add the chopped almonds and cook for a further minute or so.

4 Keep the heat low and stir in the prepared sugar syrup, taking care as the semolina may spit. Bring the mixture to the boil, stirring it constantly. When it is just smooth, remove the pan from the heat and stir in the honey.

5 Allow to cool slightly, then mix in the reserved sugar. Pour the halva into a greased and lined shallow pan, pat it down and mark into 12–16 squares.

6 Sprinkle the halva lightly with ground cinnamon and fix one almond half on each square. When set, cut up and serve.

HONEY AND PINE NUT TART

W onderful tarts of all descriptions are to be found throughout France, and this recipe recalls the flavours of the south.

INGREDIENTS

FOR THE PASTRY

225g/8oz/2 cups plain flour
115g/4oz/½ cup butter
30ml/2 tbsp icing sugar
1 egg
icing sugar, for dusting
vanilla ice cream, to serve (optional)

FOR THE FILLING

115g/4oz/½ cup unsalted butter, diced
115g/4oz/½ cup caster sugar
3 eggs, beaten
175g/6oz/⅔ cup sunflower or
other flower honey
grated rind and juice of 1 lemon
225g/8oz/2⅓ cups pine nuts
pinch of salt

SERVES 6

1 Preheat the oven to 180°C/350°F/Gas 4. Sift the flour into a bowl, add the butter and work with your fingertips until the mixture resembles fine breadcrumbs. Stir in the icing sugar. Add the egg and 15ml/1 tbsp of water and work to a firm dough that leaves the bowl clean.

2 Roll out the pastry on a floured surface and use it to line a 23cm/9in tart tin. Prick the base all over with a fork, and chill for 10 minutes. Line with foil or greaseproof paper and fill with dried beans or rice, or baking beans if you have them. Bake the tart case for 10 minutes.

3 Cream together the butter and caster sugar until light. Beat in the eggs little by little. Gently heat the honey in a small saucepan until runny, then add to the butter mixture with the lemon rind and juice. Stir in the pine nuts and salt, then pour the filling into the pastry case.

4 Bake the tart in the preheated oven for about 45 minutes, or until the filling is lightly browned and set. Leave it to cool slightly in the tin, before dusting it quite generously with icing sugar. Serve the tart warm, or at room temperature, with vanilla ice cream, if liked.

CHOCOLATE AND ORANGE CAKE

Spain is not famous for its cakes, but this light-as-air sponge, with its fluffy icing that melts in the mouth, tastes absolutely heavenly.

INGREDIENTS
25g/1oz/¼ cup plain flour
15g/½oz/2 tbsp cocoa powder
15g/½oz/2 tbsp cornflour
pinch of salt
5 egg whites
2.5ml/½ tsp cream of tartar
115g/4oz/generous ½ cup caster sugar
blanched and shredded rind of 1 orange, to decorate

FOR THE ICING
200g/7oz/1 cup caster sugar
1 egg white

1 Preheat the oven to 180°C/350°F/Gas 4. Sift the flour, cocoa powder, cornflour and salt together three times into a bowl. Beat the egg whites in a large bowl until foamy. Add the cream of tartar, then whisk until soft peaks form.

2 Add the caster sugar to the egg whites a spoonful at a time, whisking after each addition. Sift a third of the flour and cocoa mixture over the meringue and gently fold in. Repeat, sifting and folding in the flour and cocoa mixture two more times.

3 Spoon the mixture into a non-stick 20cm/8in ring mould and level the top. Bake in the oven for 35 minutes or until springy when pressed lightly. Turn upside-down on to a wire rack and leave to cool in the tin. Carefully ease out of the tin.

4 For the icing, put the sugar in a pan with 75ml/5 tbsp water. Stir over a low heat to dissolve. Boil until the syrup reaches 120°C/250°F on a sugar thermometer, or when a drop of syrup makes a soft ball when dropped into cold water. Take off the heat.

5 Whisk the egg white until stiff. Add the syrup in a thin stream, whisking all the time. Continue to whisk until the mixture is very thick and fluffy. Spread the icing over the top and sides of the cake. Sprinkle with the orange rind and serve.

Index